FINANC

Business

John Eve
BA, M.Ed., FCMA, MBIM, Cert.Ed.
North Staffordshire Polytechnic

Allister Langlois
B.Sc., BA, Cert.Ed., MBIM, AHCIMA.
Guernsey College of Further Education

Oxford University Press   1987

Oxford University Press,
Walton Street, Oxford OX2 6DP

Oxford New York Toronto
Delhi Bombay Calcutta Madras Karachi
Petaling Jaya Singapore Hong Kong Tokyo
Nairobi Dar es Salaam Cape Town
Melbourne Auckland

and associated companies in
Beirut Berlin Ibadan Nicosia

Oxford is a trademark of Oxford University Press

ISBN 0 19 832740 4

Typeset by
Katerprint Typesetting Services, Oxford
Printed in Great Britain by
Butler & Tanner Ltd., Frome

Contents

Preface

This book forms part of a series, written mainly for students of BTEC National Level Diploma or Certificate.

Each book in the series is directed towards a specific unit. However the nature of a BTEC National course is such that there needs to be integration between the separate units, and assessment will be designed to test abilities of co-ordination and use of skills across a wide spectrum.

For this reason, topics covered in each book should not be seen as specific to one book only. For instance, communication skills will be needed to communicate effectively financial information, therefore activities in the Finance book will draw heavily on this aspect covered in detail in the People in Organizations unit.

The books are written in a way that is intended to make the reader active in studying. This means that the activities in the books are not just tests of recalling facts or information: they are intended to involve the reader in activities that will enhance the learning process by involvement in tasks.

Each book covers the objectives laid down by BTEC, but reading the text alone will be insufficient. Activities are designed to be integral to the process of acquiring knowledge and then using this knowledge to tackle business problems.

J. Eve,
A. Langlois,
May, 1986.

Acknowledgements

We are grateful for the contributions to this book from Peter Williams who provided the block on Public Organizations, as well as the interview with the local authority treasurer, and also to Peter Byrne.

Anne Meredith provided the information on the work of a credit controller, and Les Ruffell of the Nationwide Building Society provided the contribution on the work of a building society manager. David Samman provided the contribution on the work of a bank manager, and advice on current accounting practice was given by Reads and Co.

We acknowledge the help of the Walsall Health Authority in providing information, of the Nationwide Building Society in allowing us to use their documentation, and also *Which* magazine for permission to reproduce material.

We are grateful to the Business and Technician Education Council for allowing us to reproduce part of the National Awards specifications in this series of books.

Carol Eve and Jane Langlois assisted in the preparation of the text. Rob Scriven at Oxford University Press provided support and guidance.

Our thanks to them all.

Introduction

It is important that you study this introduction before trying to use the book

Approach and method

This book has been written mainly for students studying for a Business and Technician Education Council (BTEC) National level award which includes the Finance unit. The BTEC award stresses the need to develop skills while studying, and hence regards study as a very active process. Simply acquiring knowledge is not enough in itself and so skills in the application of that knowledge must be developed if the award is to be really useful to the student.

A traditional textbook which simply outlines the facts which are part of the syllabus is therefore not likely to satisfy the needs of a BTEC student. A traditional textbook centres its attention on the author's or teacher's knowledge and his or her choices of how to present it. The BTEC approach is rather to centre attention on the individual needs of the reader or the student. This book provides a series of learning activities which should stimulate the reader to be involved in the learning process in an active manner. Not only is the reader required to participate in the acquisition of locally relevant and up-to-date knowledge, but activities are also provided to develop the reader's skills in applying that knowledge. The book does not even claim to provide a complete listing of all the knowledge related to the subject of finance, since the authors believe that no such listing can be appropriate to all students. It is intended instead that the activities will provide each student with guidelines for exploring and learning the basic principles of, and skills associated with, finance.

> The activities in the book are shown as in this paragraph. In many cases you will need to produce a full answer elsewhere in order to get the most out of the activity. Suggested answers or guidance for the activities is often given in the text following the activities.

Activities

This book is divided into twelve blocks. Each block in the book (except for the last one) examines an area of finance by suggesting activities which will develop knowledge and skills relevant to the BTEC Finance unit, and then provides guidance on specific financial knowledge or techniques which might be required for successful completion of the activity.

The activities are not intended to be used in their present form as BTEC assignments, but some of them may be suitably adapted for that purpose. Neither is it necessary for the student to complete every single activity in the book in order to study the course successfully. In some cases it may be more appropriate to think briefly about the activity and then, having studied the guidance section, to proceed to the next activity. If you are a student on a full-time course you would be well advised to attempt as many of the activities as possible, since you should have time for studying and you have not had experience at work of the subject matter. If you are a part-time student, your time for studying will probably be more limited, so you should select those activities from which you feel you will learn most. This will usually mean that any activity which looks difficult will provide the most effective learning. If you feel that an activity is easy and that you could complete it quickly, it probably means that you would not learn much from attempting it. Check with the guidance within the text, however, to ensure that you are not missing the point.

It is important to recognize that there are no 'right answers' to most of the set activities, and that in some cases the 'answer' consists of encouraging you to ask appropriate further questions. In addition to this, the activities will require you to make use of skills developed in the People in Organizations units and in the Organization in its Environment units.

Skills

The skills that are required for the BTEC Finance unit are concerned with being able to collect information and to use this information in a practical and useful way. In other words not just 'having knowledge' but having the ability to *use* the knowledge in a practical business situation.

Some of the skills are listed below and wherever possible they are contained in the activities that are suggested in this book. Remember that these skills are important to a whole range of activities in all the books in this series.

Learning and study skills These will be contained in all the activities and the assignments that you complete. They will be developed as you work on a variety of different tasks.

Working with others It is a skill to work with other people and to be able to respond to their attitudes and their abilities. Businesses usually contain people who have differing approaches and purposes, and an important business skill is to be able to work with others.

Communicating It is little use having knowledge or information if you cannot pass it on to others. The skill of selecting the most appropriate method of communicating is important and is developed more fully in the People in Organizations units.

Numeracy The skills in this area are concerned with feeling confident with figures and numbers. Most company reports contain detailed figures for profit and valuation of assets, and the 'users' of such information need to be familiar with the use of numbers. The skill is not just being able to compile statistics and make calculations but also to be able to communicate them effectively so as to convey their meaning.

Information gathering The business world requires data, information and statistics. Knowing where to collect the information from, and then actually doing the collecting, is a skill: its development is encouraged in the tasks set in this book.

Information processing The skill in processing information, once gathered, is important. Processing may mean using computers or other information processing technology, or it may simply mean writing on a sheet of paper with a pen. Choosing the best method of processing is important as a skill, as of course is the skill of actually doing the processing.

Identifying and tackling problems Problem solving is a skill. Identifying the problem is also a skill. The tasks set in this book will help to identify problem areas of finance and suggest methods and techniques for solving financial problems. Being aware of a problem can sometimes be as important as being able to offer a solution.

Design and visual discrimination We all respond to the environment in which we live and work. The way information is presented to us is important, and can influence our response to it. An awareness of the importance of design skills is vital to people in organizations. Design includes documentation design as well as other aspects of business, such as the working environment.

The skills described above are very active. To develop them you need to be involved in activities and tasks that require you to collect information, use the information, and use a whole range of other resources to aid your studies. This book is one resource designed to help this process.

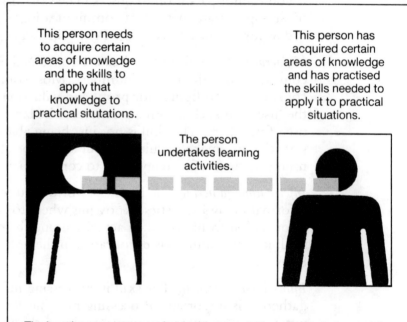

This person needs to acquire certain areas of knowledge and the skills to apply that knowledge to practical situtations.

This person has acquired certain areas of knowledge and has practised the skills needed to apply it to practical situations.

The person undertakes learning activities.

The learning process must lead to the acquisition of knowledge and the development of skills. *Learning activities* are designed to achieve this. In a learning activity the student must ask questions, practise skills, and be able to communicate knowledge to others.

Summary of how to use this book

1 Select a block to study. The authors believe that the blocks follow a logical development, but if your course is following a different sequence then there is no reason why you should not change the order of the blocks. Block 1 is intended as the best introduction to the course so we would strongly advise you to attempt it first.

2 Work through the activities alone or together with colleagues on your course. If you need guidance on any particular aspect of the activity, you should find it immediately following the activity. If you don't, then remember that the index should help you to find the information you require.

3 If you find any aspect of the work puzzling, then be sure to ask for help from your lecturer or teacher, somebody at work, or one of the organizations involved in finance which are mentioned in the text.

If you follow the advice above all should go well, so we will delay you no longer. Start Block 1 as soon as you can!

General Objectives and Indicative Content

BTEC courses at National Level are designed to promote the development of skills in students that can be used in the business world. These skills need to be developed and applied within a course framework. This framework comes in the form of 'General Objectives and Indicative Content' in each unit.

This book covers all the indicative content of the finance unit: the following list of general objectives is amplified by the content used to achieve those objectives.

The Blocks where the coverage is achieved is indicated below:

A Recognize the importance of, and be able to apply, accounting and financial analysis techniques in relation to personal finance

Sources of personal finance	Block 1
Revenue and capital expenditure in personal finance	Block 1
Personal taxation	Block 1
Other deductions from gross pay	Block 1
Opportunity cost, individual objectives and personal finance	Block 1
Cash planning and personal cash flow	Blocks 1 and 3
The role of the accountant in giving advice on personal finance	Block 1

B Explain the various sources of finance which are available to fund different types of organization

Internal and external sources for social, public and private organizations	Blocks 4 and 11

C Outline the development, purpose and function of accounting

The role of the accountant in private practice	Blocks 1 and 12
The role of the accountant in an organization	Blocks 1 and 12
Methods of collecting financial data	All blocks
Main source documents for financial data	Blocks 1, 3, 6, 7, 9 and 10
Potential users of financial information	All blocks

The development of accounting in   All blocks
   response to the changing needs of
   organizations, starting as a simple
   recording function and expanding to
   provide financial information for a
   variety of users
Documents for the control of cash, e.g.   Block 3
   bank statements, cash books, petty
   cash books

D Describe and explain accounting concepts and conventions

The uses and limitations of accounting   Block 1
   concepts and conventions as they
   affect the recording of financial data,
   e.g. methods of stock valuation and
   depreciation

E Appreciate the construction of financial statements for private, public and social organizations in accordance with accounting concepts

Simple final accounts	Block 4
Equivalent public sector revenue and expenditure statements	Block 11
Club accounts	Block 10
Revenue and capital expenditure in organizations	Blocks 2 and 9

F Explain and illustrate the needs of management and others for financial information for planning, control and decision taking

Planning the financial needs of an organization or project	Blocks 8 and 9
Budgeting and planning procedures for both capital and revenue	Blocks 1 and 9
Cost control	Blocks 1, 5 and 9
Cost behaviour and its uses, marginal costing and break-even analyses	Block 6
The use of specific financial techniques for decision making, e.g. Project Appraisal and DCF techniques	Block 9

G Interpret financial information in order to measure performance against the perceived objectives of the organization

Absolute and relative measures of performance	Block 4
Variation in financial objectives between different organizations	All blocks
Different interpretations placed on given data by interested parties	All blocks

H Appreciate the influence of finance on organizational decision making and its relation to other factors involved in management decisions

Financial, human and legal pressures on managers	All blocks
The social and ethical implications of financial decisions related to people's behaviour, working conditions and morale	Block 7
Examples of occasions when financial factors will be secondary in decision making	Block 6

Each of these objectives can be linked with the specific objectives in the other books in the series and the other BTEC units. General objective H above, for example, should be seen as having relevance across a whole range of other objectives both within the Finance and other units.

An important feature of both teaching and learning in BTEC courses, is to attempt to see a study of business as only being possible if you are prepared to look for links between the content of separate units and learning materials.

Block 1
Personal Finance and Financial Principles

Introduction

As somebody coming to the study of finance for the first time, what do the documents on the next page mean to you? Anything? Nothing? Any study of finance must introduce you to documents and records used constantly by individuals, businesses, and public sector organizations. The documents themselves are less important than the principles behind them. Financial documents are linked within an organization to form a logical progression. They are related to each other in such a way that they form part of an overall system which is used for planning, recording and monitoring the financial activities of the organization.

Financial systems may be used by individuals or by the largest of organizations, but many financial principles apply to all of them. The BTEC Finance unit may be the only formal financial study you ever undertake, or it may be the start of many courses in finance and accountancy. Either way, we want to start with you and your finances so that you can see that financial principles have an application.

The individual or the family makes use of finance as a resource. A resource is a means of supplying a want and so without finance in some form the wants which are the basis of economic life in a modern society cannot be satisfied. Goods and services are paid for with money (in most cases). Whether one is buying a new stereo, a car, a bar of chocolate, a haircut, a ticket to a football match, or an insurance policy, money is still used.

The result of this is that the individual or the family needs a source of finance from which to satisfy their economic wants. There are various sources of finance in the same way as there are various uses for it and the first learning activity in this course is designed to make you think about finance as a flow of resources in and out of the family unit, and as a provider of stock items for the household.

BALANCE SHEETS at 31st MARCH 1985

	Notes	The Group 1985 £m	The Group 1984 £m	The Company 1985 £m	The Company 1984 £m
Fixed assets					
Tangible assets	13	305.5	299.3	16.0	14.8
Investments	14	67.6	60.3	313.1	279.8
		372.9	359.6	329.1	294.6
Current assets					
Stocks	18	874.5	813.1	0.3	0.2
Debtors	19	258.1	237.8	903.2	937.1
Short term deposits		166.7	57.4	154.4	54.0
Cash at bank and in hand		32.5	19.8	18.4	10.5
		1,331.8	1,128.1	1,076.4	1,001.8
Creditors: amounts falling due within one year	20	(294.2)	(204.4)	(141.9)	(£120.2)
Net current assets		1,037.6	923.7	934.5	881.6
Total assets less current liabilities		1,410.5	1,283.3	1,263.6	1,176.2
Creditors: amounts falling due after more than one year	22	(305.9)	(103.0)	(293.6)	(93.2)
Provisions for liabilities and charges	24	(67.4)	(67.9)	(1.7)	(2.5)
		1,037.2	1,112.4	968.3	1,080.5
Capital and reserves					
Called up share capital	26	181.6	181.6	181.6	181.6
Revaluation reserve	27	—	—	(34.6)	135.9
Other reserves	27	62.3	232.0	96.8	96.2
Profit and loss account	27	770.3	680.9	724.5	666.8
		1,014.2	1,094.5	968.3	1,080.5
Attributable reserves of related company	28	23.0	17.9	—	—
		1,037.2	1,112.4	968.3	1,080.5

J M Connell, Chairman
R S Temple, Director

17th July 1985

YEAR ENDED 31st MARCH 1985

	Notes	1985 £m	1985 £m	1984 £m
Turnover	2 and 3		1,274.3	1,134.1
Excise duty			(342.1)	(327.3)
Turnover excluding excise duty			932.2	806.8
Cost of sales			(619.9)	(551.8)
Gross profit			312.3	255.0
Distribution costs		(28.8)		(27.8)
Administrative expenses		(50.0)		(45.8)
Other operating income (charges)		(0.3)		0.2
			(79.1)	(73.4)
Trading profit	3 and 4		233.2	181.6
Share of profit (loss) of related company			4.2	(1.1)
Income from investments	7		9.0	7.2
Interest	8		(13.6)	1.9
Surplus on realisation of investments			3.4	2.0
Profit on ordinary activities before taxation			236.2	191.6
Taxation	9		(102.9)	(63.3)
Profit on ordinary activities after taxation			133.3	128.3
Extraordinary items less attributable taxation	10		(7.5)	(9.5)
Profit for the year			125.8	118.8
Dividends	11		(54.4)	(49.5)
Transfer to deferred taxation			—	(60.3)
Profit retained			71.4	9.0
Retained by				
The Company		60.2		73.9
Subsidiary companies		6.1		(59.9)
Related company		5.1		(5.0)
			71.4	9.0
Earnings per share	12		36.71p	35.35p

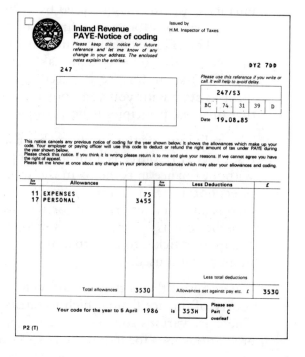

Different kinds of financial document.

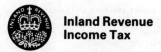

Inland Revenue
Income Tax

This leaflet shows the income tax rates and thresholds and the personal allowances which have effect for the income tax year 1986–87 (ending 5 April 1987), as a result of the Finance Act 1986.

Rates of tax

The basic rate of income tax is reduced to 29%.
The higher rates of tax (40%-60%) are unchanged. The starting point for the 40% rate has been increased from £16201 to £17201 taxable income and the other higher rate thresholds have also been raised. The new bands compared with the 1985-86 bands are as follows:

		1985-86 Bands £	1986-87 Bands £
Basic Rate	29%	1-16200	1-17200
Higher Rates	40%	16201-19200	17201-20200
	45%	19201-24400	20201-25400
	50%	24401-32300	25401-33300
	55%	32301-40200	33301-41200
	60%	Over 40200	Over 41200

Personal allowances

The personal allowances are increased as shown in the following table:

Allowance	1985-86 £	*Increase* £	1986-87 £
Single Person	2205	130	2335
Married Man	3455	200	3655
Wife's Earned Income	2205	130	2335
Age - Single Person*	2690	160	2850
Age - Married Man*	4255	250	4505
Additional Personal	1250	70	1320
Widow's Bereavement	1250	70	1320

*The income limit for the full age allowance will be increased to **£9400** (previously £8800).

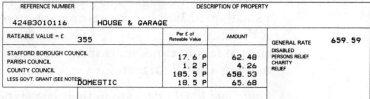

STAFFORD BOROUGH COUNCIL

RATE ACCOUNT FOR THE PERIOD 1st APRIL, 1986 TO 31st MARCH, 1987

Rates are due on demand, but the Council allows settlement by TWO HALF YEARLY PAYMENTS, provided the first payment is received by 31st MAY and the second payment by 15th OCTOBER. If the first payment is not received by 31st MAY the TOTAL DUE becomes payable IMMEDIATELY.
The Council also accepts applications from ratepayers to pay by MONTHLY INSTALMENTS, and payments under this Scheme are due on the 10th of EACH MONTH, normally between May and February (details of this scheme are given overleaf).

FAILURE TO CONFORM TO THE PAYMENT INSTRUCTIONS WILL LEAD TO RECOVERY PROCEEDINGS FOR THE BALANCE OF THE YEAR'S RATES.

REFERENCE NUMBER	DESCRIPTION OF PROPERTY
42483010116	HOUSE & GARAGE

RATEABLE VALUE = £ 355	Per £ of Rateable Value	AMOUNT	GENERAL RATE	659. 59
STAFFORD BOROUGH COUNCIL	17. 6 P	62. 48	DISABLED PERSONS RELIEF CHARITY RELIEF	
PARISH COUNCIL	1. 2 P	4. 26		
COUNTY COUNCIL	185. 5 P	658. 53		
LESS GOVT. GRANT (SEE NOTES) DOMESTIC	18. 5 P	65. 68		
			TOTAL DUE	659. 59
		Address of property rated if different		

OR OCCUPIER

```
          AMENDED BILL DUE TO PAYMENT ARRANGEMENT CHANGE
             7 17 13 0483 0010 1 3   PROPERTY REFERENCE   (PLEASE QUOTE)
    ACCOUNT   ) UPPER TRENT DIV.WESTPORT ROAD,BURSLEM,
    ENQUIRIES
    ONLY TO   ) STOKE ON TRENT ST6 4JT,TEL:STOKE 817631

                                        1/0007    Date 290885

    H
PLEASE NOTIFY
ANY CHANGE IN                                    DIRECT DEBIT
NAME OR ADDRESS
                                                 STATEMENT

                                                 OWNER REF.
ADDRESS OF SUPPLY
(IF DIFFERENT)

CHARGE DESCRIPTION      RATEABLE VALUE    CHARGE RATE PER ( R V      CHARGE
BILLED AMOUNTS STILL O/S                                            86.98

                                                 TOTAL CHARGES
IMPORTANT NOTICE
The details shown above are for                £        86.98
information only. No further action is
necessary on your part as there is an    1ST PAYMENT OF    £21.76        FOR
existing Banker's Authorisation covering
these charges and requests for payment   ON  1ST OCT 1985          INFORMATION
will be made to your bank automatically.
In the unlikely event of our making        3 PAYMENTS OF    £21.74        ONLY
an error you can obtain an immediate     ON 1ST OF EACH SUBSEQUENT MONTH
refund from your bank.

ACCOUNT ENQUIRIES

       Enquiries concerning this statement should be made to the divisional office whose address and telephone number are shown above
       Please quote your property reference on all correspondence

   SERVICE ENQUIRIES & EMERGENCIES see telephone directory under the heading WATER
```

Which of the documents on this and previous pages are you already familiar with?

Throughout this block on personal finance we shall use three examples of people with different patterns of income and expenditure.

1 *Sarah Kidd* is nineteen years old. She lives at home with her parents and is unemployed apart from a part-time job, four hours a week, on Sunday morning at a local newsagent. She attends college one day a week but apart from that her main interests are music and sport, being a keen member of the local athletic club.

2 *John and Mary Settle* are in their early thirties. They have two children aged seven and eight, and John works as a salesman for a garage. They are buying their house and run a small car. Mary has a part-time job two evenings a week at the local pub and any spare cash which does not go on normal family expenses is spent on their joint interest in running a small caravan for weekend and holiday trips.

3 *Philip and Ethel Older* are in their late sixties. Philip has recently retired from his job in local government and they are looking forward to enjoying their new-found leisure time. They live simply but enjoy an occasional holiday and share an interest in local history, frequently attending classes in the area. They have a daughter and two grandchildren who live close by and visit them frequently.

Activity 1	*Where does your money come from?*

Taking each of the above three examples in turn, list all possible sources of finance for each individual or family. This list should include all possibilities, even those which are not necessarily normal or even strictly legal!

Personal income

The activities in this block dealing with personal finance all recognize that there are a number of possible sources of income for an individual or a family. Your answer to Activity 1 may have included any of the following:

Wages or salary

Income from trade or profession for self-employed people

Pension income

Loans from banks or other sources

Inherited funds

Interest received on money invested

Winnings on lotteries, football pools, premium bonds or other forms of gambling

State benefits, such as unemployment pay, family income supplement, sickness benefits or supplementary benefits

Illegal income, such as theft, fraud, or tax evasion (we strongly recommend that you should avoid this type of income, but it is, for some people, a form of income, at least until they get caught!)

Activity 2	Activity 2 *Where does your money go?*

Taking each of our examples in turn (Sarah Kidd, the Settles and the Olders), list all the types of spending which you might expect them to make. When you have constructed a rough list classify the spending in two ways:

1 Types of expenditure which are common to all three examples.

2 Types of expenditure which account for a large part of the total and which occur less frequently than normal running expenses.

Personal expenditure

Your answer to Activity 2 may well have included many more different types of example than those for personal income. You should, however, have included some of the following in your answer:

Rent or mortgage payments

Everyday expenses, such as food, heating or transport

Occasional large items of expenditure such as a car, a stereo, or a home computer

Savings

Taxation

Many of these are easily understood in that they are the sort of spending that you may make yourself, but the tax system and other deductions from earnings often cause confusion. Later in this block we will look in more detail at various ways in which money is deducted from personal income before we ever receive it.

As you have now seen when you completed Activities 1 and 2, personal finance can be seen as a **flow of money** for the individual or the family.

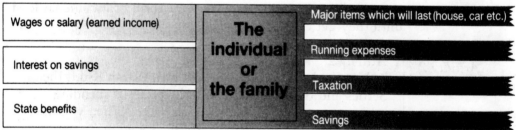

Sources of funds		**Applications of funds**
Wages or salary (earned income)		Major items which will last (house, car etc.)
Interest on savings	The individual or the family	Running expenses
State benefits		Taxation
		Savings

Personal finance as a flow of money.

The following activities should help you to understand the overall pattern of income and expenditure for a household and to see the way in which particular items of expenditure require special techniques for the planning and management of finance.

Activity 3	Running a household budget

John Settle (already mentioned as an example above) earns about £8500 per year. His monthly salary varies slightly as he is paid a basic wage but also earns commission on sales made. A typical pay advice for one month's work is shown below. Mary is paid £18 per week for her work; she is paid in cash each evening and all tax and deductions are paid through John's employment.

							NAME		
HOUSE	**RATE**	**AMOUNT**	**BONUS**	**CODE**	**AMOUNT**	**GROSS WAGE**	J. SETTLE		
SALARY		£708.33	COMMISSION	29	124.22	£832.55	6006.07 694322 28/11/86		

INCOME TAX	**SUPERAN.**	**NAT INS.**	**N.I. NUMBER**		**TAX CODE**		
103.20	39.50	55.43	YL 66/02/65/N		364	SUPER GARAGE plc PAY ADVICE	

GROSS PAY TO DATE	**TAXABLE PAY TO DATE**	**SUPERANNUABLE PAY TO DATE**	**TAX TO DATE**	**SUPERANNUATION TO DATE**	**PAY POINT**	**CHECK NO.**	**DATE**
£6660.40	£6344.40	£6660.40	763.65	296.25	6006	694322	28/11/86
N.I. TO DATE					50p ROUND UP		
426.78		**TOTAL DEDUCTIONS** £198.13			**NET PAY** £634.42		

A typical monthly pay advice for John Settle.

Mortgage payments are £148 per month and the family also pays life insurance premiums of £32 per month to cover the family should anything happen to John as the main wage earner.

John and Mary have found it increasingly difficult to manage their money month by month as the children get older and begin to make a bigger impression on the family budget. They have been attracted by the idea of a budget account run by their bank so that the family estimate all their standard expenses for the year, divide by twelve, and make a monthly transfer from the current account. The bank then allows the customer to overdraw temporarily on the budget account so that cheques for all household expenses can be written without worry and the account should balance out at the end of a year.

In addition to the regular expenses already mentioned, John and Mary want to make provision for the following household expenses to be paid out of the budget account as shown on pages 16–17:

1 Electricity

The account shown below is for the spring quarter last year and is payable in June. An analysis of other accounts shows the following pattern of electricity costs:

Quarter	Percentage of annual cost
Winter	38
Spring	22
Summer	13
Autumn	27

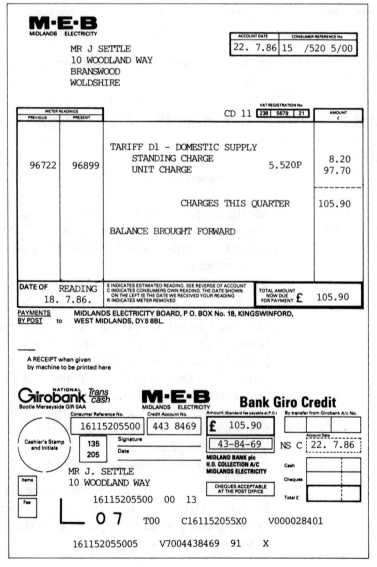

Last year's spring electricity account for John and Mary Settle.

2 Coal

The house has a system of coal-fired central heating and John likes to keep a steady stock of coal. They expect to spend about £55 every month on coal except in June and August when they will not need to buy any.

3 Telephone

The telephone bill arrives quarterly, the first of the year being due in February, and is fairly evenly spread throughout the year. Last year they spent a total of £92 on phone bills.

4 Rates

The local authority rates for the house work out at £27.50 per month. As usual these are payable half yearly in advance in April and October.

5 Insurance

John pays life insurance premiums as mentioned above and in addition to this he has the following insurance premiums to pay:
a Car insurance which was £87 last year, due on 12 April each year.
b House insurance payable to the building society in September of each year. Last year's premium was £63.
c House contents and personal effects insurance of about £38 payable in March.

6 TV Licence

The licence fee is due in October.

7 Clubs and societies

John and Mary pay the following subscriptions to clubs:
a Mary's Badminton club subscription due in October and costing £24.
b John's Cricket Club subscription due in April and costing £26.
c The Caravan Club subscription due in May at £17.

You are required to prepare

a A cash budget for the year showing the likely overdraft limit required for the budget account. An explanation and example of the layout for such a document is shown below.

b A letter to the bank manager explaining your proposal and including reference to the cash budget which you have prepared.

c A set of questions which you, as an employee of the bank, might ask the Settles when examining their proposal. Try to get them to justify the figures they have produced.

Cash budgets

All individuals and organizations need to plan their cash flow to have enough money available to meet their various needs from time to time. The arithmetic involved in calculating how much money you expect to have at any given time is fairly simple but it helps if you use a standard layout to display your plans. When planning cash flows, it is the timing of receipts and payments which is most important; all movements of money must be taken into account.

The table at the top of the next page should help you to see how a cash budget for an individual's personal income and expenditure might be presented. Similar types of budget are used for businesses. Note that in accounting it is a convention that brackets are used to show a negative figure.

In each week **total receipts** are added to the **opening cash balance** and **total payments** deducted to find the **closing cash balance**. This amount then becomes the **opening cash balance** for the next week.

Clearly the individual in the example is going to hit some problems in Week 4 of June unless he or she can change some plans, or unless he or she has a very understanding bank manager who will grant overdraft facilities!

Cash budget

	June Week 1	Week 2	Week 3	Week 4	July Week 1	Week 2
Opening cash balance	64	109	102	132	(125)	(199)
Receipts						
Salary	136	136	130	140	140	168
Bank interest						48
Sale of moped		35				
Family income supplement	9			9		9
Total receipts	145	171	130	149	140	225
Payments						
Mortgage				158		
Electricity				46		
Gas				35		
Rates				27		
Living expenses	82	82	82	82	82	82
H.P. Payment				40		
Petrol	18	18	18	18	18	18
Car insurance		78				
Car tax					90	
House insurance					24	
Total payments	100	178	100	406	214	100
Closing cash balance	109	102	132	(125)	(199)	(74)

Deductions from income

Activity 4

Deductions from gross income
You will have noticed on the pay advice shown for Activity 3 that the net pay received by John Settle was considerably less than his gross earnings.
a Write a letter to John explaining in as much detail as possible how the amount payable for each deduction from gross earnings is calculated, where the money

goes, and any ways in which John Settle may influence
the amount of these deductions.

b Would you expect the deductions from the gross
incomes of Sarah Kidd, and of Philip and Ethel Older,
to be any different from those of John and Mary
Settle? Draw up a table of comparison showing ways
in which the pattern and amounts of deductions would
differ for each of our examples. The table should
include comparison of the amount of each deduction
and reasons why they differ from our other examples.

Income tax

Income tax is usually payable under the Pay As You Earn
scheme (PAYE). All employed people are liable to pay
income tax under this scheme, the exact amount depending
on their personal circumstances. Each person is given a tax
code and the employer calculates the amount of tax to be paid
using this code. You would be well advised to collect a leaflet
of guidance on personal tax matters from your local tax
office, as this will explain in detail how your tax liability is
being calculated and list the current rates of tax and personal
allowances. Some recent rates of tax and allowances are
shown on page 11. Rates of tax and personal allowances often
change as a result of the Chancellor of the Exchequer's annual
budget. Rates of tax and allowance vary depending on the
amount the government wishes to raise each year through
direct taxation.

National insurance

In addition to Pay as You Earn income tax, employees also
pay national insurance and this is similarly deducted from
their wages at source. The amount of such insurance
payments (called **primary contributions**) affects an
individual's entitlement to state pension and, in certain cases,
unemployment benefit. National insurance tables are used to
calculate the appropriate deduction as a percentage of
earnings. Married women are entitled to pay at a reduced rate
and pensioners are not liable as long as earnings do not exceed
a lower earnings limit.

Employers are also required to make an earnings–related
contribution (the **secondary contribution** in respect of each
employee). Records are maintained by the employer in

respect of all national insurance and Pay as You Earn deductions; monthly payments should be made to the Collector of Taxes.

Pension contributions

On John Settle's pay advice (see page 15), we can see that he has paid to a superannuation scheme. This is a private scheme operated by his employers, and is in addition to the state-run pension scheme. Not all firms operate these schemes, so employees will not have a 'firm's pension' when they retire. Those who contribute to a company pension or super-annuation scheme, however, will receive an additional pension on retirement dependent upon the amount of the payments they have made into the scheme.

Financing personal expenditure

| Activity 5 | *Large items of expenditure* |

Large items of expenditure
You might have noticed that expenditure by an individual or family may be classified into two groups:

a Day-to-day running expenses for food, light and heat, transport, etc.
b The occasional purchase of a major item such as a house, a car, or expensive item of electrical equipment.

In financial language the day-to-day expenses are generally known as **revenue expenditure** while the purchase of large items which will continue to be used for some time is known as **capital expenditure**. These terms are more generally applied to the activities of businesses and organizations but may also be used in relation to personal finance, in that the process of spending money on major items is somewhat different from that of spending money on everyday items. We shall use the term capital expenditure when related to personal finance to mean the purchase of a house, a car, a large item of electrical equipment, or anything else which will last for some time and costs more than about one week's pay.

In order to study the process of making capital expenditure you are asked to examine this question in relation to something you would like to buy.

a Select an item which would cost you significantly more than one week's income and which you would like to investigate the cost of (e.g. a stereo, a car, a camera, etc.)

b Research the prices of a range of similar items and draw up a table of prices, special features, and advantages and disadvantages of each.

c Research and discuss different sources of finance for such a purchase, e.g. cash savings, hire purchase, a bank loan, credit cards, etc., and outline their advantages and disadvantages, including the costs and benefit of each method.

d Imagine that you are trying to convince somebody else of the wisdom of your final choice of item and method of payment. Assemble the material in a file presented in such a way as to justify your decision. Your decision will of course be influenced by factors other than purely financial ones and you should include these factors in your argument.

Communicating to another person the reasons for your decision to purchase a particular item may be the most difficult part of the exercise. Remember that not everybody has had your advantage of studying a finance course; you should therefore present the information in the simplest form possible. If you make it too simple however you run the risk of leaving out important points or of having to answer a whole series of difficult questions. Remember that simple tables of figures and diagrams often explain things better than words, and these, together with other communication skills you are developing elsewhere in your course, should be evident in the presentation of your results.

If you complete all aspects of Activity 5 you should find that your file of information has the following features:

1 The choice of a consumer item is rarely a simple matter. For the examples mentioned in the activity a wide range of

The TVs we tested

	target price £ [6]	size h×w×d (cm)	main features	connections	other features on set	remote control	picture quality	sound quality
Ferguson 22D2 (UK) [2]	320	44×65×39		S [1]	N	abcnrsu	▨	☐
Ferguson 51A2 (UK) [3]	400	42×61×48	F	HS [1]	BMN	abcnrstuv	▨	☐
Fisher CFB 2110STX (Japan)	480 (50)	47×64×48	EFT	AHISV	BM	brstux	▨	☐
GEC C2296H (UK) [4]	330	51×64×48			N	abcorux[7]	▨	▨
Hitachi CPT 2246 (UK) [13]	370	48×63×50		AHIRV	BN	abrsu	▨	▨
ITT CT 3425 (W Germany) [5]	360	45×63×41		AH	NO	abrsux[7]	▨	▨
ITT CT 3435 (W Germany)	390	40×59×47	F	AHI	NO	abrsux[7]	▨	☐
Mitsubishi CT 2101 TX (UK)	445	48×52×48	EFT	HS	MO	acnrsux	▨	▨
Panasonic TX 5500 (UK) [8]	390	45×67×47	E		N	bcstuvx	▨	☐
Panasonic TXC22 (UK)	530 (40)	51×51×50	EFT	AHISVX	BM	bcstuvx	▨	▨
Philips 4829 (Belgium)	450	44×66×47	EFT	HSX	N	Babrsuvx	▨	▨ [9]
Sony KV2215UB (UK) [10]	400 (70)	45×62×41		AHIVX	B	cnrstuvx[7]	▨	☐
Toshiba 212T (UK) [11]	430	51×52×48	EF	HS	BMN	abrsux	▨	▨
Zanussi 22ZA374 (Italy) [12]	350	45×63×42		HS	N	0abcnrsux[7]	▨	☐

Key to Table

Connections (see text)
A = audio output
H = headphones socket
I = audio and video inputs
R = RGB input
S = SCART connector
V = video output
X = external loudspeakers sockets

Main features
E = teletext
F = flatter, or full, squarer tube
T = stereo sound

Other features
B = bass and treble tone controls
M = removable tinted screen
N = stand (with castors and video shelf) supplied
O = single tone control

Remote control
All can select the programme you want, adjust
volume, and mute the sound
a = reset levels adjustable
b = brightness
c = contrast
n = indicator on set that command received
o = off switch
r = reset
s = on/standby
t = TV/audio-video selector
u = colour
v = video recorder controls
x = teletext controls
B = bass and treble tone controls
O = single tone control

KEY TO RATINGS	▨ ▨ ☐ ▨ ■ best ← → worst

An example of a product comparison by *Which* magazine.

products is available, all having different features and prices. Convincing yourself that you have made the right choice should be difficult enough, let alone trying to convince somebody else! It may help however to write out a list showing the price of each model and tabulating the features which it includes. The consumer magazine *Which* is a good source of information on such matters and makes extensive use of tables to display the prices and features of products tested.

2 Your research should also have revealed that if one has to borrow money for a major purchase rather than spend some savings, there is a wide variety of sources from which funds may be obtained. Banks, finance companies, and credit card firms are all in business to lend money to the public as profitably as they can. In the same way as you 'shop around' for the items you are buying, you should also 'shop around' for the cheapest and most appropriate source of finance.

Sources of personal credit

Hire purchase

Hire purchase (HP) agreements are those where a purchaser enters into a contract with a financing company to hire the item on sale in the shop or showroom. Hire charges, including interest payments on the total cost of the item, are usually made on a monthly basis and on completion of the final payment ownership changes from the finance company to the customer. During the period when HP payments are being made, the item belongs to the finance company.

Credit sale

This differs from HP in that ownership passes immediately to the purchaser, but payment for the item is delayed, and is often made by instalments. Interest is then charged on the amount of money outstanding at any time, making the total cost greater than if the sale had been for cash. The Consumer Credit Act (1974) limits this type of agreement to transactions between £50 and £1500.

Credit cards

Sometimes referred to as 'plastic money', credit cards have become a normal method of payment for goods and services. Potential customers may apply to the organizations offering credit cards, such as Access, American Express, Visa, or the clearing banks. If granted permission to use a card they will be given an upper limit for credit and can purchase up to this amount monthly provided that the previous balance of the account has been cleared. Payment is made to the company, usually on a monthly basis for the amount shown on the statement. If payments are spread over later months, then interest is charged.

Building societies

The traditional role of the building society, that of collecting savings from investors and lending it to borrowers in the form of mortgages at a higher rate of interest, is now changing as more consumer services are offered.

As the banks have now started to offer mortgage facilities, so building societies have started to offer consumer credit facilities. Services offered by some societies include cheque books, foreign currency provision, credit cards, cash dispensers and standing order payments.

Bank loans

Most banks have loan account facilities for customers, with differing rates of interest payable, dependent on the terms of the loan, the repayment period, the frequency of instalments and security offered.

Overdraft facilities are granted to some customers and they may then draw more money from their current accounts than they have paid in, allowing the balance to become negative or 'in the red'.

As part of Activity 5 you may have visited banks, building societies or finance companies and asked what services are available. If you have not already done this, it is worth doing so as most banks offer special services to young people.

Each method of borrowing has its advantages and dis-advantages relating to period of time for repayment, arrange-ments in case of default on payments, frequency of instalments, and most important of all, price, in this case the true rate of interest. Laws for the protection of borrowers require that the true rate of interest should be clearly displayed in any agreement and this figure should be of major interest to anybody signing an agreement to borrow money.

Interest rates are complicated. Banks and building societies compete, and part of this competition is shown in the rates of interest either charged on loans or offered on deposits.

Also 'advertized' rates need to be checked carefully, particu-larly when they compare rates offered by different organizations. Are they calculated on the original loan amount or the outstanding balance? Is it an average rate? Pay careful attention to details of this kind.

The consumer magazine *Which* also publishes periodic reviews of personal finance. An example is shown on the following pages comparing different forms of personal bank account. Take careful note of the features which they compare, such as interest rates, charges, and facilities offered. *You must realize however that the information given was only appropriate to February 1986 and is constantly changing.*

Table 1: Bank current account charges

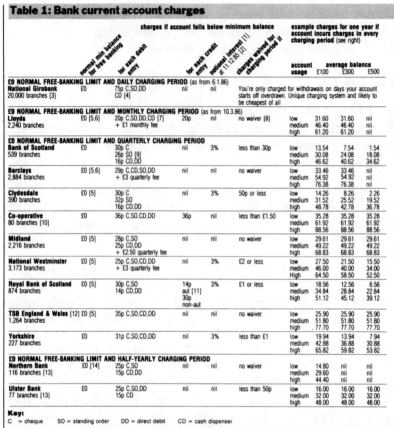

	normal min balance for free banking	for each debit entry	for each credit entry	notional interest [1] at 11.12.85 [2]	charges waived for charging period if	charges if account falls below minimum balance — example charges for one year if account incurs charges in every charging period (see right)		account usage	average balance £100	£300	£500

£0 NORMAL FREE-BANKING LIMIT AND DAILY CHARGING PERIOD (as from 6.1.86)

National Girobank 20,000 branches [3]	£0	75p C,SO,DD CD [4]	nil	nil		You're only charged for withdrawals on days your account starts off overdrawn. Unique charging system and likely to be cheapest of all					

£0 NORMAL FREE-BANKING LIMIT AND MONTHLY CHARGING PERIOD (as from 10.3.86)

Lloyds 2,240 branches	£0 [5,6]	20p C,SO,DD,CD [7] + £1 monthly fee	20p	nil	no waiver [8]	low medium high		31.60 46.40 61.20	31.60 46.40 61.20	nil nil . nil

£0 NORMAL FREE-BANKING LIMIT AND QUARTERLY CHARGING PERIOD

Bank of Scotland 539 branches	£0	30p C 26p SO [9] 16p CD,DD	nil	3%	less than 30p	low medium high	13.54 30.08 46.62	7.54 24.08 40.62	1.54 18.08 34.62
Barclays 2,884 branches	£0 [5,6]	29p C,CD,SO,DD + £3 quarterly fee	nil	nil	no waiver	low medium high	33.46 54.92 76.38	33.46 54.92 76.38	nil nil nil
Clydesdale 390 branches	£0 [5]	30p C 32p SO 16p CD,DD	nil	3%	50p or less	low medium high	14.26 31.52 48.78	8.26 25.52 42.78	2.26 19.52 36.78
Co-operative 80 branches [10]	£0	36p C,SO,CD,DD	36p	nil	less than £1.50	low medium high	35.28 61.92 88.56	35.28 61.92 88.56	35.28 61.92 88.56
Midland 2,216 branches	£0 [5]	28p C,SO 25p CD,DD + £2.50 quarterly fee	nil	nil	no waiver	low medium high	29.61 49.22 68.83	29.61 49.22 68.83	29.61 49.22 68.83
National Westminster 3,173 branches	£0 [5]	25p C,SO,CD,DD + £3 quarterly fee	nil	3%	£2 or less	low medium High	27.50 46.00 64.50	21.50 40.00 58.50	15.50 34.00 52.50
Royal Bank of Scotland 874 branches	£0 [5]	30p C,SO 14p CD,DD	14p aut [11] 30p non-aut	3%	£1 or less	low medium high	18.56 34.84 51.12	12.56 28.84 45.12	6.56 22.84 39.12
TSB England & Wales [12] 1,264 branches	£0 [5]	35p C,SO,CD,DD	nil	nil	no waiver	low medium high	25.90 51.80 . 77.70	25.90 51.80 77.70	25.90 51.80 77.70
Yorkshire 227 branches	£0	31p C,SO,CD,DD	nil	3%	less than £1	low medium high	19.94 42.88 65.82	13.94 36.88 59.82	7.94 30.88 53.82

£0 NORMAL FREE-BANKING LIMIT AND HALF-YEARLY CHARGING PERIOD

Northern Bank 116 branches [13]	£0 [14]	25p C,SO 15p CD,DD	nil	nil	no waiver	low medium high	14.80 29.60 44.40	nil nil nil	nil nil nil
Ulster Bank 77 branches [13]	£0	25p C,SO,DD 15p CD	nil	nil	less than 50p	low medium high	16.00 32.00 48.00	16.00 32.00 48.00	16.00 32.00 48.00

Key:
C = cheque　　SO = standing order　　DD = direct debit　　CD = cash dispenser

Example charges for one year

The charges shown assume your balance falls below the free-banking limit at least once in each charging period. Examples for average balances of £100, £300 and £500, and for the following account usage:

Account usage	Cheque/cash dispenser	Standing order/ direct debit
Low	50 (25 of each)	24 (12 of each)
Medium	100 (50 of each)	48 (24 of each)
High	150 (75 of each)	72 (36 of each)

With banks that charge for credits, we allowed for 24 of these (12 credit transfer, 12 cheques paid in). We assume debits and credits distributed evenly through year.

[1] Yearly rate, calculated daily
[2] All information shown as at 11.12.85, other than charges for Lloyds (which come into effect from 10.3.86) and National Girobank (6.1.86)
[3] At post offices
[4] In practice 0p – you can't withdraw from a dispenser if overdrawn
[5] Free banking for students even if overdrawn, subject to size of overdraft or bank's prior agreement. Definition of 'student' may be quite wide eg to include student nurses, articled clerks
[6] Or an average balance of £500 (times when you're in the red are counted as a zero balance)
[7] Charges for each day dispenser used, not each transaction
[8] No waiver of transaction charges, but interest on overdraft waived if under £1
[9] Fixed charge of 10p irrespective of balance – plus, if you go into the red, an extra charge of 16p
[10] Plus 690 Handybanks in Co-op stores to cash Co-op cheques, pay money in etc, plus 3,290 cash-a-cheque points in Co-op stores
[11] Non-automated credits include cheques, cash, standing orders paid into your account. Automated credits include salary paid by credit transfer
[12] Charges shown are for TSB England & Wales. Free-banking limit is £0 in all TSBs and each has its own transaction charges. TSB Northern Ireland is the cheapest, but has a half-yearly charging period, followed by TSB Scotland (quarterly charging period)
[13] Branches in Eire not included
[14] Or an average balance of £200 (counting times when you're in the red as a minus amount)

Table 2: Current accounts which pay interest

● = feature available on this account	cheque book	cheque card	cash card	standing orders	direct debits	special credit card facilities	minimum initial investment	yearly rate of interest [1]	interest credited	minimum deposit & withdrawal	charges
Adam & Company Adam Current Account (031-225 8484)	●	[2]	[3]	●	●	Free Diners Club card [4]	no minimum	below £1,000 : nil [12] £1,000 to £4,999 : 6.66% £5,000 plus : 8.24%	quarterly	no minimum	none, if balance £250 or above for whole charging period. Otherwise, 35p C,SO; 30p CD,DD
Allied Dunbar Dunbar Master Account (0793 28291)	●	●		●	●	Dunbar Visa card [7]	£2,500 [8]	below £2,000 : 5.64% £2,000 plus : 8.3%	monthly	no minimum	5 transactions per month free. Others 30p each. £2 per month standing charge
Co-operative Cheque & Save (01-626 6543)	●	●	●	●	●		no minimum	below £500 : nil £500 to £2,499 : 7.29% on whole balance 9.33% on amount in excess of £2,500	quarterly	no minimum	£3 per month standing charge
HFC Trust & Savings Current Account Plus [10] (01-236 8391)	●	●		●	●		no minimum	6.16%	monthly	no minimum	none, even when account is overdrawn
Provincial Trust Current Account (061-928 9011)	●	●		●	●		£1	below £500 : nil £500 plus : 6.5% on whole balance	quarterly	no minimum	none, even when account is overdrawn
Save & Prosper Classic High Interest Bank Account (0708 66966)	●		●	●	●	Visa Classic card [9]	£500	below £5,000 : 5.12% on first £500 and 8.44% on excess up to £5,000 £5,000 plus: 8.44% on whole balance	daily	no minimum (but cash deposits not normally acceptable)	£2 per month if month-end balance is less than £1,000
Save & Prosper Premier High Interest Bank Account (0708 66966)	●	[6]	●	●	●	Visa Premier card [9]	£1,000	below £1,000 : nil £1,000 plus : 8.44% on whole balance	daily	no minimum (but cash deposits not normally acceptable)	£2 per month if month-end balance is less than £5,000
Western Trust & Savings Chequebook Savings [11] (Freeline 9427)	●	●	●	●	●		£5	7.4% £1,000 plus [5] : 8.88% £10,000 plus [5] : 9.52%	quarterly	no minimum	40p per withdrawal

[1] As at 11.12.85. Allows for the effect of interest being paid more than once a year and being credited to account where this happens. Rate is for non-taxpayers and basic rate taxpayers
[2] £250 cheque guarantee facility
[3] Royal Bank of Scotland 'Cashline' card

[4] Can be used to cash cheques free at NatWest branches
[5] Balance required for whole quarter
[6] £75 cheque guarantee facility
[7] Visa card settled automatically from Master Account at account month-end. 1% transaction fee on cash advances
[8] As from 1.1.86

[9] No transaction fee on cash advances of £100 or more. Cash debited from account immediately
[10] Guaranteed overdraft limit automatically arranged
[11] Overdraft facility limited to £100 over 7 day period
[12] Notional interest of 3% on balances under £1,000 to offset against charges

Table 3: Deposit cheque accounts

● = feature available on this account	cheque book	cheque card	cash card	standing orders	direct debits	minimum initial investment[8] [1]	yearly rate of interest [1]	interest credited	minimum deposit & withdrawal [2]	charges
Adam & Co High Interest Cheque Account (031-225 8484)	●					no minimum	£0 to £499 : 5.09% £500 to £4,999 : 6.66% £5,000 plus : 8.24%	quarterly	no minimum	10 cheques per quarter free. Others 35p each
Aitken Hume Monthly Income Account (01-638 6011)			● [3]			£1,000	below £1,000 : nil £1,000 plus : 8.57%	monthly	£250	none
Allied Arab Bank High Interest Bearing Current A/c (01-283 9111)	●			●	●	£5,000	below £2,000 : 4.97% £2,000 plus : 8.94%	monthly [10]	no minimum	6 debits per quarter free. Others 50p each
Bank of Scotland Money Market Cheque Account [4] (031-346 6000)	●	●				£2,500	below £2,500 : 4.05% £2,500 plus : 8.53%	monthly	£250	9 cheques per quarter free. Others 50p each
Barclays Prime Account (0604 252891)	●			● [5]		£2,500	below £2,500 : 4.04% £2,500 plus : 8.51%	quarterly	£250	6 cheques per quarter free. Others 50p each
Britannia/Cater Allen High Interest Current Account (01-588 2777)	●			● [9]	● [6]	£2,500	below £500 : nil £500 plus : 8.54%	monthly [10]	£250	none
Charterhouse Japhet Premium Account (01-248 3999)	●					£2,500	below £2,500 : nil £2,500 plus : 8.32%	monthly	no minimum	15 cheques per quarter free. Others 50p each
Citibank Savings Money Market Plus (01-741 8000)	●					£2,000	below £1,000 : 8.00% £1,000 plus : 9.75%	monthly	£50 withdrawals	none
Cheque Plus			●			no minimum	below £500 : 6.5% £500 plus : 8.0%	quarterly	no minimum	none
Clydesdale Bank High Interest Cheque Account (041-248 7070)	●					£2,000	below £2,000 : 5.79% £2,000 plus : 8.51%	quarterly	£200 withdrawals	none
Edward Manson & Co Cheque Deposit Account (01-631 3313)	●					£1,000	8.97%	half-yearly [10]	no minimum	none
Lloyds Bank High Interest Cheque Account (01-626 1500)	●	●	●	●	●	£2,500	below £2,500 : 5.09% £2,500 plus : 8.51%	quarterly	no minimum	3 withdrawals per quarter free. Others 50p each
Lombard North Central Cheque Savings Account (01-409 3434)	●					£250	below £250 : nil [7] £250 to £2,499 : 6.841% £2,500 plus : 8.392%	when rates change and at least half-yearly	no minimum	First book of 20 cheques free. Subsequent cheques 25p each
M & G/Kleinwort Benson High Interest Cheque Account (0245 51651)	●					£2,500	below £900 : nil £900 plus : 8.54%	quarterly [10]	£200	none
Midland Bank High Interest Cheque Account (0742 20999)	●					£2,000	below £2,000 : 5.83% £2,000 to £9,999 : 8.24% £10,000 plus : 8.56%	quarterly	£200 withdrawals	none
Oppenheimer Money Management Account (01-236 9362)	●					£1,000	below £1,000 : nil £1,000 to £9,999 : 8.28% £10,000 plus : 8.48%	quarterly	£200	none
Provincial Trust Money Market Cheque Account (061-928 9011)	●			●		£1,000	8.95%	monthly [10]	£250	none
Royal Bank of Scotland Premium Account (031-557 0201)	●	●	●	●	●	£2,500	below £2,500 : 4.56% £2,500 plus : 8.47%	quarterly	no minimum	35p C,SO 20p CD,DD
Save & Prosper Deposit High Interest Bank A/c (0708 66966)	●			● [3]	● [3]	£1,000	below £1,000 : nil £1,000 plus : 8.44%	daily [10]	£250	none
Schroders Special Account (0705 827733)	●					£2,500	below £10,000 : 8.54% £10,000 plus : 8.74%	monthly	£250	none
Western Trust & Savings High Interest Cheque Account (Freefone 9427)	●					£2,000	below £1,000 : nil £1,000 to £4,999 : 8.77% £5,000 plus : 8.98%	quarterly	£200 withdrawals	none

[1] Rate as at 11.12.85. Rate is for non-taxpayers and basic rate taxpayers. Allows for the effect of interest being paid more than once a year and being credited to account, where this happens
[2] Cheques below minimum level may be paid by some institutions, but they may charge for doing so. In some cases

one cheque per month below minimum may be allowed
[3] £250 minimum payment waived
[4] Henderson Unit Trust Management (01-638 5757) have a similar account (also with Bank of Scotland)
[5] One free standing order per month to current account
[6] For TSB Trustcard account only

[7] Rates below assume interest credited half-yearly
[8] Some accounts may be closed or transferred to another account if balance falls below opening balance
[9] One free standing order per month for any amount
[10] Monthly income option (may be subject to minimum balance requirement)

Table 4: Other bank deposit accounts with current account facilities

	cash card	standing orders	direct debits	min initial investment	yearly rate of interest [1]	instant access without loss of interest	interest credited	charges
Bank of Scotland Keycard Deposit	●	●	●	£1	below £500 : 3.39% £500 to £1,999 : 4.92% £2,000 plus : 7.03%	yes	half-yearly	10p SO
Clydesdale Autocash	●	●	●	£1	below £500 : 3.28% £500 to £999 : 4.81% £1,000 plus : 5.96%	yes	half-yearly	32p SO
Lloyds Cashpoint Deposit	●			1p	5.83%	yes on CD withdrawals. Otherwise 7 days' interest lost, unless notice given	half-yearly	none
Midland Saver Plus [2]	●			£100	£100 to £249 : 6.4% £250 to £500 : 6.92% £500 to £999 : 7.45% £1,000 plus : 8.03%	yes	quarterly	none
NatWest Deposit Account	●			£1	5.83%	no – 7 days' interest lost on all withdrawals, unless notice given	half-yearly	none
Northern Bank Saver Plus	●			£100	£100 to £249 : 5.75% £250 to £499 : 6.25% £500 to £999 : 6.75% £1,000 to £1,999 : 7.25% £2,000 plus : 7.75%	yes	annually	none
Royal Bank of Scotland Cashline Deposit	●	●	●	£1	below £500 : 2.99% £500 to £999 : 4.48% £1,000 plus : 5.98%	yes	annually	40p SO, 20p DD
Deposit Account	●			£1	6.11%	no – 7 days' interest lost on cash dispenser withdrawals; also on other withdrawals unless notice given	quarterly	none
TSB England & Wales Service Account [3]		●	●	5p	2.0%	yes	annually	50p SO,DD

[1] Rate as at 11.12.85. Rate is for non-taxpayers and basic rate taxpayers. Allows for effect of interest being credited to
account more than once a year, where this happens
[2] Transfers to and from current account may be made
through cash machines
[3] TSBs Scotland and Channel Islands have own accounts

Table 5: Building society accounts with banking features

● = feature available on this account

	account name	cheque book	cash card	standing orders	direct debits	minimum initial investment	minimum to keep account open	yearly rate of interest [1]	charges
Abbey National 678 branches (contact local branch)	Cheque-Save [2]	●	●		● [3]	£100	£1	£1 to £2,499 : 5.58% £2,500 to £9,999 : 9% £10,000 to £24,999 : 9.25% £25,000 plus : 9.73%	none
	Share Account		●			£1	£1	7.12%	none
Alliance & Leicester 453 branches (0273 775454)	ReadyMoney Plus [4]			●		£1 [12]	£1	7.12%	none
	BankSave Plus – see Table 6								
Anglia 399 branches (0604 495353)	Share Account [5]		●			£1	£1	7.12%	none
Bradford & Bingley 250 branches (0274 568111)	Share Account		●			£1	£1	7.00%	none
	Pay Plan (and Plan & Save) [15]	●	●	●		£50 [18]	£1	6.5% (Pay); 8.00% (Save)	none
Bristol & West 163 branches (0272 29222)	BlueCard		●			£1	£1	7.12%	none
Britannia 241 branches (contact local branch)	Moneymaster Account		●			£1	£1	7.12%	none
Cambridge 7 branches (0223 315440)	CBS Cashcard		●	● [7]		£250	£1 [16]	7.38%	none
Chelsea 51 branches (contact local branch)	Capital Shares	●	●			£1,000	£1 [19]	£1 to £2,499 : 9.10% £2,500 to £9,999 : 9.55% £10,000 plus : 9.8%	up to 50 cheques per year free. Others 50p each
Dunfermline 39 branches (0383 720842)	Everyday Share		●	● [20]		£1	£1 [16]	7.12%	none
Halifax 713 branches (contact local branch)	Cardcash [6]		●		●	£1	£1	£1 to £1,999 : 7.12% £2,000 plus : 9.2%	none
Leeds Permanent 480 branches (contact local branch)	Pay & Save	●	●	●	●	£100	£1	7.12%	none
Market Harborough 4 branches (0858 63244)	Cash Centre Account	●	●			£100	£50 [9]	7.12%	none
Nationwide 527 branches (contact local branch)	FlexAccount	●	●		● [11]	£25	£1	below £25 : 7.00% £25 to £1 999 : 7.25% £2,000 plus : 9.00%	none
	Ordinary Share Account				● [11]	£1	£1	7.12%	none
Peterborough 41 branches (0733 51491)	Cash Counter Account		●	● [14]		£1	£1 [13]	7.12%	none
Portman 46 branches (0202 292444)	Portman Link		●	● [14]		£100	£100	below £100 : 7.00% £100 to £1,999:8.00% £2,000 plus : 9.00%	none
Swindon Permanent 3 branches (0793 21108)	Paid-Up Share [4,10]			●		£1	£1	7.38%	none
Town & Country 70 branches (contact local branch)	Moneywise	●		● [17]		£250	£1	£1 to £2,499 : 5.75% £2,500 to £9,999 : 9.00% £10,000 to £19,999 : 9.50% £20,000 plus : 9.80%	50p per debit when balance below £250
Woolwich Equitable 401 branches (contact local branch)	Cashbase		●			£1	£1	7.25%	none
Yorkshire 159 branches (0274 734822)	Cashkey		●	●		£1	£1	7.12%	none

[1] Interest rate as at 11.12.85. Rate is for non-taxpayers and basic rate taxpayers. Allows for the effect of interest being paid more than once a year and being credited to the account, where this happens
[2] Investments of £10,000 or more are in City Cheque-Save – interest rates as shown
[3] For Amex and Co-op Visa card bills only
[4] Withdrawals and deposits may be made at post offices
[5] Payments and cash withdrawals in some Northampton shops using EFTPOS – see *Which?* December 1985, p570
[6] Bill payment service and transfers between accounts through cash machines (see *Which?* Inside Story, September 1985, p389)

[7] Only to pay Cambridge mortgages
[8] Six standing orders only
[9] Cash cards available with weekly withdrawal limits of £50, £100 and £200. To use cash dispenser, balance must be three times weekly limit. Balance to keep account open is the same as weekly limit
[10] Standing orders available on most Swindon accounts
[11] Direct debits to Nationwide mortgages and LEB only
[12] But £100 minimum investment required to qualify for cash card
[13] £100 balance to use cash dispensers
[14] Limited to 10 standing orders
[15] Accounts can be linked. One automatic transfer a month

free from Pay Plan to Plan & Save. Automatic transfers back to Pay Plan as necessary to cover withdrawals, but interest rate reverts to Pay Plan (6.5%) if there are more than six withdrawals a year
[16] But £250 minimum balance required to withdraw cash from cash dispensers
[17] Five standing orders only
[18] But £1 if salary is to be paid into account
[19] Account may be transferred to ordinary share account if balance falls below £1,000
[20] To certain other Dunfermline accounts

A *Which* comparison of banking services.

The accountant and the accounting profession

Activity 6	*Seeking advice on personal finance*

Seeking advice on personal finance
On some occasions everyone needs to seek the advice of an expert in the matter of personal finance. For this task you are to imagine that you have just started work with a Citizen's Advice Bureau. Knowing that you are attending a Business Studies course the manager of the bureau asks you to write a leaflet outlining possible sources of advice. You should include in the leaflet a list of names and addresses of people and organizations in your area who may be able to provide advice and a table or diagram indicating the type of advice provided by each source and any associated costs. Remember that firms of accountants, banks and insurance companies all supply professional advice on financial matters. Names and addresses of local sources are available in the Yellow Pages of your telephone directory.

When seeking advice on financial matters, one perhaps obvious source is an accountant. Often accountants are thought of as fairly anonymous people who complete the accounts for businesses. This to some extent is true, but there are different types of accountants working in a wide variety of businesses carrying out different sorts of activity. The most successful organizations often spread accounting information widely amongst employees so that everybody is aware of financial objectives and constraints and is better informed and more motivated.

At the beginning of this century an accountant was only concerned with accounting; he was qualified professionally and worked on the accounts of businesses. With the growth and development of commercial activity, coupled with changes in manufacturing processes, the business world has become more complex, and the demands on the accounting profession are much greater. For this reason specialization within accounting has been considerable. Nowadays the accounting profession has four major 'chartered' bodies offering professional accounting qualifications. Each specializes in particular aspects of accounting, although all of them have common areas that are examined in their professional examinations.

Some accountants are self-employed and offer their services to businesses and private individuals. These accountants operate singly as 'sole practitioners' or else they work for large accounting firms often offering worldwide services. Other accountants operate in industry and commerce providing specialist knowledge to organize and operate financial control in the businesses which employ them.

Qualified accountants are entitled to be members of the major accounting bodies:

The Institute of Chartered Accountants
The Chartered Association of Certified Accountants
The Chartered Institute of Management Accountants
The Chartered Institute of Public Finance and Accounting

In addition to these, the Association of Accounting Technicians is an organization of people working in accounting. A member of this association is not a professional accountant but has a qualification which is relevant to work in the accounting field and gives the member certain exemptions from professional accounting exams should he or she choose to pursue accounting studies. Within accounting there are different specialisms.

Auditing

Auditors check and verify the documents and statements produced by other accountants or owners of businesses to ensure that they give a 'true and fair view' of the business in question. An audit is a detailed examination of the financial statements of a business, involving detailed searches of and checks on the records kept. The auditor is often a member of a professional accounting firm whose competence and integrity give the required credibility to the financial information reported. An 'audit' is a legal requirement for public limited companies.

Taxation

Businesses and individuals have to pay tax on income. Income is represented mainly by profits in the case of businesses, and wages or salaries in the case of individuals. The tax payable differs both in method of payment and means of calculation. Corporation Tax is payable on company profits, and income tax on personal earnings. Some accountants specialize in giving advice on taxation matters, often so as to minimize the amount payable, by using specialized knowledge of the law and taxation system.

Computing

Most businesses and some individuals use computers to keep records of transactions, and to process those transactions by extracting financial statements from them. The systems used vary enormously, depending on the size of the firm and the detail involved in the records. Accountants often specialize in this area of data recording although they are more concerned with the quality of information provided than with the technical details of how the computers work.

Management accounting

This branch of accounting helps with the internal management of all types of business. Analysis of business activities will reveal which areas are the most profitable. Products and areas of activity can be assessed by managers only if their financial contribution to the firm is known. Rational decisions can then be made by managers and it is the function of the management accountant to provide the information on which these decisions should be based.

Costing is really part of management accounting, and is concerned with providing detailed costs for products, departments and operations. See Block 5 for more information about costing.

In this book the emphasis is on finance in the sense of a resource to individuals and businesses and also as a means of measuring the success of businesses. Accounting techniques for detailed recording of financial information will not be a major area of consideration in remaining sections.

However, accounting is the major form of recording financial events and transactions and some consideration needs to be made of accounting methods and procedures and also the rules and conventions that accountants follow when producing accounting statements.

At the end of financial periods, usually a year, accounts will be produced. Profit and Loss accounts to show the profit (or loss) made will need to show the revenues earned and the costs incurred. Without detailed records throughout the year this will not be possible. Similarly a Balance Sheet is needed to show what assets are owned by the business and what debts and liabilities it has. Again without records being kept this kind of financial statement will not be possible. You will learn more about such financial statements in Block 4.

To be able to produce these sort of statements, valuations need to be made, careful judgement exercised and records need to be kept. The users of accounting and financial information will rely on these statements being 'true and fair', so each accountant must attempt to follow general accounting rules and principles so that all statements are produced following the same general principles of design, layout and valuation.

Standard accountancy practice

Much of accountancy consists of a series of conventions. Conventions in accounting are agreed rules relating to layout and calculation of figures. These conventions mean that accountants can communicate with each other in an agreed language. The rules are designed to give a 'true and fair view' of the financial status of the organization, although as we have already seen, figures may always be subject to different interpretations. A company's profit which might be regarded as excessive by the employer's union may be interpreted as being low and inadequate by the company's shareholders. Such a conflict on interpretation does not make the preparation of accounts according to a standard and agreed method any less valid.

Layout

At the simplest level accountants follow a convention of layout which places the descriptions, or details, of each item on the left-hand side of the page, and a series of columns for figures on the right-hand side. Within these columns sub–totals are calculated in the left-hand columns and successive levels of total are then transferred to the right or more 'senior' column. This convention is used throughout accounting statements in an effort to make them neat, clear and informative. An example of a typical accounting layout is shown at the top of the next page.

Fixed and Current Assets are different types of item owned by an organization. When added together they are described as Total Assets. The accounting layout enables the reader to see the sub-totals for each type of asset, and the overall total, clearly and without further calculation.

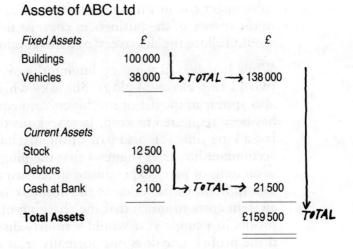

Assets of ABC Ltd

Fixed Assets	£		£
Buildings	100 000		
Vehicles	38 000	→ TOTAL →	138 000
Current Assets			
Stock	12 500		
Debtors	6 900		
Cash at Bank	2 100	→ TOTAL →	21 500
Total Assets			£159 500 TOTAL

Accounting concepts and conventions

As well as the simple conventions of layout and presentation, accountants follow a number of guiding principles. You will see these in action throughout your study of finance, but to make you aware of them consider now the case of Mrs Jane Salisbury who runs a small restaurant.

Jane Salisbury has just bought a new microwave oven. She saw it advertized in a closing down sale of an electrical supplier's shop and, as it was still in the shop on the actual afternoon when it was due to close, she managed to buy it at half the manufacturer's recommended price. The following week her accountant, Karen Bennett, is asking her about the value of the business' assets and she tells her about the bargain. Karen advises her to value it at the figure which it actually cost her rather than the recommended price. This is a standard accountancy practice called the **cost concept**, which states that all assets should be kept on the books at cost unless a substantial reason exists for them to be revalued. Such a revaluation might occur in the case of land and buildings which, in addition to being a very secure asset, tend to rise in value.

The decision to give the lower value to the oven also follows a basic convention of **prudence** or **caution**. Accountants always err on the side of undervaluing benefits rather than risk overvaluing. By following this convention any subsequent rise in value may be treated as a pleasant surprise to the owner of the business in contrast to the shock which would follow the discovery of an overvaluation.

While Jane was in the shop buying the oven she also bought two 13 amp electrical plugs. She asks whether these should also appear in the list of machinery and equipment which she has been requested to keep. Jane reckons that as a plug should last a long time it is also part of the machinery. The accountant however suggests that the plugs should be treated as an item of petty expenditure since their combined value is unimportant to the value of the business as a whole. Unless an item costs so much that the charging of its full cost against profits in a single year would seriously distort the meaning of those profits, one does not normally treat it as a fixed asset. This follows the convention of **materiality**, whereby only long-lasting items of significance are included in the detailed accounting records of assets.

Jane feels that her assistant in the restaurant, Paul, who does much of the cooking, is the most valuable asset to the business. She asks Karen whether his reputation as a chef can be represented in the same way in the book value of the business. The **money measurement concept**, however, states that since something as uncertain and intangible as reputation cannot be given an easily agreed value, then it should not appear in the books. This should be noted when interpreting the value of many businesses whose employees may be their greatest asset.

Among the other financial questions which Jane discusses with the accountant, she is concerned about a particular job which she undertook about a month ago. The local rugby club organized a dinner for fifty people, taking over the whole restaurant for the evening. Despite assurances that she would receive the money within a week, the cheque still has not appeared. With the financial year end now arriving Jane is worried about whether she should count the profit made that night as part of the profit for the year. Karen, the accountant, assures her that the **realization concept** states that profit occurs when the goods or services change hands and that the transfer of cash is not relevant to this calculation. A similar principle applies to unpaid bills for expenses. If, for example, an electricity bill for power consumed during the financial year now ending is unpaid, its cost should still be counted against revenue in the period when the electricity was consumed. This is known as the **accruals** or **matching principle**, meaning that costs and revenue should be matched with the period in which they occur.

Proprietors of small businesses often use their own cars for business purposes and Jane is no exception to this. The garage sends her account to the restaurant and after it is paid the cost is shared out between the business accounts and her own personal expenditure, reflecting the split between her business and private use of the car. The **business entity** principle states that any business has a separate identity from that of its owners and that this type of division of costs should therefore be made.

Another worry which Jane Salisbury has relates to the car. The accountant last year advised her that the car should last about five years and that one fifth of its cost should be charged as an expense each year. Because prices have changed rapidly, she now wants to change this method and take account of current car prices. Karen advises her against this on the basis of the **consistency principle** which states that once a decision has been made regarding the method of allocating costs this should not be changed, unless it is absolutely necessary, so that figures from different financial periods may be fairly compared. Karen will also assume, when preparing the accounts, that the business is going to continue indefinitely, that it is a **going concern** and, should it reach a stage of being gradually or suddenly closed down, then special accounting techniques would be used to deal with this.

Activity 7

Make a list of the nine principles used by accountants and explain each one in a single sentence to help you to remember its meaning.

Conclusion

On completion of this block you should have discovered a lot about the sources and applications of personal finance, and about some of the decisions which an individual or family must make when managing the household budget. You may choose to repeat some of the activities in relation to your own finances. Let's hope that you are not too horrified by the results! Many of the lessons you have learned here may be applied equally well to the finances of organizations, as you will see in the remainder of the text, and you may also find that some of the more sophisticated techniques discussed later can be applied to certain aspects of personal finance.

In both personal and organizational finance a constant process should be taking place:

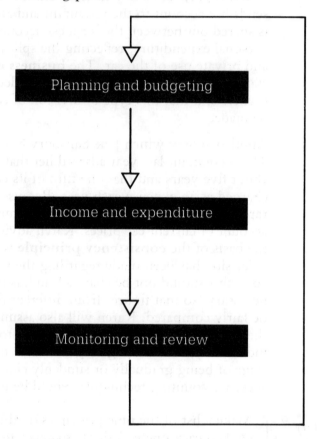

By following this process a degree of *control* will be achieved and financial problems will be seen in context as just one of a wide range of considerations to be taken into account in personal and business decision making.

As you learn more about finance you will find that the following financial principles are applied in many situations: the cost concept, prudence (or caution), materiality, the money measurement concept, the realization concept, the accruals or matching principle, the business entity principle, and the consistency principle. In making financial decisions, you will always be well advised to follow these principles.

Block 2
Finance and Large Items of Capital Expenditure

Introduction

A fixed asset in an organization is an item which the organization expects to keep for a long time to assist in its activities, such as buildings, vehicles and machinery. Such assets are only added to organizations occasionally, and cost a lot in relation to the overall finances of the organization. There are two ways to acquire use of such assets: by buying them or by renting or leasing them from the owner.

Fixed assets: to rent or to buy?

In terms of personal finance one of the most important decisions all of us make is related to housing. For most people accommodation is one of the main forms of spending throughout their lives and it therefore deserves special attention. The decision whether to rent or buy is also one faced by businesses and other organizations in relation to buildings, and nowadays to a whole range of fixed assets, such as vehicles and machinery. The purpose of this block is to introduce you to some of the considerations involved in such a decision by examining a series of situations in which individuals or firms are acquiring the use of a fixed asset and making choices about the ways in which they can gain that use.

House purchase or rental?

Activity 1	Everybody needs housing of some sort and assuming that they have a certain level of income there are a number of choices open to them. We shall examine and compare just two possibilities, whether to rent or whether to buy. Imagine that you need as a minimum a

home with two bedrooms, a kitchen, bathroom and
lounge. Find out from your local newspaper and estate
agents how much it would cost
a to rent such a flat or house,
b to buy such a flat or house.

Property prices vary considerably in different parts of the
country so it is impossible to give any guidelines on the sort
of prices you might have discovered while doing Activity 1.
What will be clear, however, is that hardly anybody will be in
a position to buy a house or flat outright, so they will be
obliged to borrow the money in order to spread the cost of
purchase over a long period of time.

Activity 2   Having discovered the price of a typical small house or
flat in your area, imagine that you have about 10% of
that purchase price to put towards the purchase and that
you now wish to borrow the rest.
a Find out from your local banks and building societies
   how much per month at current rates of interest it
   would cost you to borrow that amount, and over what
   period you could borrow it. Make a list of any other
   costs you think you should take into account when
   making this decision.
b What are the advantages and disadvantages of
   borrowing over a shorter or longer period?
c What information would you expect to supply to the
   bank or building society in order to persuade them to
   make the loan?
d What rules do lenders and lending institutions impose
   on borrowers regarding the use of money? For
   example, could you use part of your building society
   loan to buy carpets and curtains?

The costs of renting or purchasing

Mortgages, or loans secured against a property, are usually
granted for a period of between ten and twenty-five years. If
you are young and buying a property for the first time, you
will probably be advised to take the loan over as long a period
as possible. Interest rates on these loans are expressed in a
number of different ways, but the easiest way to compare
them is to see how much you have to pay out each month.

Providing you are comparing loans taken over the same period, this will show you exactly which is the cheapest source of finance. Depending on the area of the country in which you are living, and the type of property you have examined, you will find that there are sometimes considerable differences between the cost of renting and the cost of purchase. You should also have noted that if you own a property you have to maintain and repair it, whereas, if you rent it, maintenance and repairs are usually done by the landlord. Arrangements for the payment of rates and other household expenses also vary and should have appeared on your list of other costs to take into account.

When renting a property there is little or no initial cost except that most landlords expect rent to be paid in advance. When buying a property, a number of expenses are incurred immediately, such as a lawyer's fee, an administration charge on the mortgage, stamp duty, etc. Thus, quite apart from the cost of furnishing the house and setting up with carpets and curtains, a large lump sum is needed to proceed with the initial purchase.

Long-term or short-term borrowing?

If you decide that purchasing is the right decision for you, and that the money must be borrowed, your next problem will be to settle on a period over which to spread the loan. Mortgages on houses are usually granted for periods of between ten and twenty-five years. When looking at the relative costs and benefits of different repayment periods you should have considered some of the factors listed below.

Long-term borrowing (more than 20 years)

Advantages	*Disadvantages*
Lower monthly repayments	Greater overall amount paid
Gains maximum benefit from tax system	Longer period before ownership
	Risk of changes in interest rates for longer period
Real value of repayments declines during inflationary times	

Short-term borrowing (less than 15 years)

Advantages	*Disadvantages*
Quicker ownership	Fewer tax benefits
Less interest paid overall	Higher monthly repayments
Less risk of interest charges	Less benefit from falling real value of repayments during inflationary times

Obtaining a loan from a bank or building society

When approaching a bank or building society for a loan, they will require a large amount of information from you about both the property and your personal circumstances. Shown on pages 41–6 are typical application forms for a mortgage loan, and your answer to Activity 2c should have included some of the details shown on the forms.

The forms shown are from one particular building society. Banks have a similar system for obtaining information from potential borrowers.

Mortgages are of different types. Repayment mortgages are those where a capital sum is borrowed, and monthly repayments include capital and interest. In the early years the interest portion of each payment is high. As the period of repayment continues a greater proportion of the capital is paid off with each repayment.

Usually borrowers take out a 'mortgage protection policy' to cover their lives, and guarantee the payment of the mortgage for their dependants.

Endowment mortgages involve covering the amount of a loan with an endowment life assurance policy, which will pay off the loan when it matures at the end of the mortgage term. If a borrower dies before the end of the repayment period, the mortgage is paid off in full. There is no need for separate insurance cover.

In addition to life cover assurance, most lenders (banks or building societies) require other forms of insurance to be taken out, specifically on the buildings covered by the mortgage.

As you will see from the building society forms, information is needed for the Inland Revenue, because mortgage interest is 'allowable' for tax purposes, with repayments being made that have allowed for income tax and are therefore lower than they would have been if they did not qualify for tax relief.

Nationwide Building Society

Issuing Branch/Agency	For office use only
	Proposal Fee £ _____
	Receipt No. _____
	Date _____
	A/c No. _____ / _____

Mortgage Application

Please complete in **BLOCK CAPITALS** and return to the issuing office with the appropriate fee and the tear-off portion of the Property Insurance form. If you require any assistance in completing your application, please contact your nearest branch.

1. Full Name of first Applicant _____

   Mr/Mrs/Miss*

   Date of Birth _____ Nationality _____

2. Full Name of second Applicant _____

   Mr/Mrs/Miss*

   Date of Birth _____ Nationality _____

3. Address for Correspondence _____

   _____ Post Code _____ Daytime Telephone No. _____

4. **Address of Property to be Mortgaged** _____

   _____ **Post Code** _____

   (a) Will the entire property be used for your own occupation as a dwelling house?   YES/NO*

   (b) If NO, specify portion to be let, rental and whether tenancy is regulated or controlled

   _____

   _____

5. Please state the full name(s) of any person, **age 17 or over**, who is not included as a mortgage applicant but who is expected to be occupying the mortgaged property with the applicant(s). (In England, Wales and Northern Ireland, all adults who will occupy the property at the time of the advance (other than borrowers) will be required to sign the Society's Form of Consent to Mortgage.)

   _____

   _____

6. Name and address of (a) Vendor/Builder* _____

   (b) Selling Agent _____

7. Please enclose key, or give details of convenient time for inspection. If key is not available, please give address and daytime telephone number where key can be obtained.

   _____

   _____

8. Name and address of your Solicitor _____

   _____ Post Code _____

   *Delete as applicable.

PROPERTY DETAILS

9. Type of property:

   1. House/Bungalow/Town House*   2. Flat/Maisonette/Tenement (Scotland)*   3. Other (specify)
      Detached/Semi Detached/Terraced*   Purpose built/Converted/over commercial premises*   _____

10. Indicate the area of land included in the purchase price, if more than one acre.   _____ acres

11. Please indicate number of:

Living rooms	Bedrooms	Bathrooms	WC's	Kitchens	Garages	Garage space	Others (specify)

12. Walls are made of _____ Roof is made of _____

13. The Property is FREEHOLD/LEASEHOLD/FEUHOLD (SCOTLAND)* Approximate age of property _____

    Amount of ground rent/chief rent/feu duty*   £ _____ pa   Years of Lease left _____

    Rateable value of property (if known)   £ _____ pa   Rates payable   £ _____ pa

    Service Charge (if applicable)   £ _____ pa   Services provided _____

14. Details of any additions or alterations which you propose making to the property immediately after completion of purchase

    _____

    _____

    If a local authority grant is being obtained, state Amount £ _____   Type _____

MORTGAGE DETAILS

15. (a) **Purchase Price** £_____ **Advance required** £_____ Term _____ years

    (b) Are you borrowing any part of your deposit?   YES/NO*

    If YES, please give details _____

    (c) If purchase price includes any extras (existing property - carpets, curtains, cooker, etc; new property - central heating, or
        other optional items), give details _____

    _____

    (d) Are you purchasing under a Shared Ownership Scheme?   YES/NO*

       Is this the Do It Yourself Shared Ownership (DIYSO) Scheme?   YES/NO*

       If, DIYSO, which Housing Association is involved?

       State the initial percentage of equity to be purchased _____%

       District Valuers Valuation £ _____ (Not if DIYSO)

16 Is there a National House Building Council Guarantee?   YES/NO*
    NOTE: When the answer to 16 is "YES" it will be a condition of any mortgage granted that NHBC cover during the guarantee period
    should be the maximum available.

17. If a new property, will the builder require the advance by instalments?   YES/NO*

18. If land is being purchased separately, please give   Price of land £ _____, Cost of building £ _____

19. If you have been saving under the Government Homeloan Scheme do you wish to apply for assistance?   YES/NO*

20. Do you wish to repay your loan with the aid of an endowment policy?   YES/NO*
    If YES, do you want the Society's help in arranging an endowment policy?   YES/NO*
    If not, please enclose details of any endowment policy you propose to use.

21. If your proposed mortgage is not to be fully covered under the endowment basis, the Society will arrange for you to receive,
    without obligation, a quotation for life assurance to repay the outstanding balance of the loan in the event of your death.

    Please indicate below whether you are a non-smoker (ie. have not smoked cigarettes within the last 12 months) as you may be
    eligible for a discount on premiums. Cigar and Pipe smokers are deemed non-smokers.

    First Named Applicant   Smoker/Non-Smoker*

    Second Named Applicant   Smoker/Non-Smoker*

    *Delete as applicable

PERSONAL DETAILS　　(Strictly Private and Confidential)

| Applicant Named in Question 1. | Applicant Named in Question 2. |

22. Address _____

Post Code _____　　　Post Code _____

23. Marital Status _____

State ages and relationships of persons dependant on you for support:

24. Name and address of employer (include department from which we may, if needed, confirm earnings)

Occupation _____

Employed there since _____

Basic Earnings　　£ _____ pw/pm/pa*　　£ _____ pw/pm/pa*

Regular Overtime　　£ _____ pw/pm/pa*　　£ _____ pw/pm/pa*

Regular Bonus　　£ _____ pw/pm/pa*　　£ _____ pw/pm/pa*

Regular Commission　　£ _____ pw/pm/pa*　　£ _____ pw/pm/pa*

　　　　　Total　　£ _____ pw/pm/pa*　　£ _____ pw/pm/pa*

If possible please produce current payslips or Form P60.

25. If you are self employed, please give name and address of business.

Nature of business _____

How long have you been so engaged? _____

Please supply copies of audited accounts for the last three years, or the name and address of your accountant.

26. Details of any other income

27. Name and address of banker

Bank A/c No. _____

28. If you are already an investor with the Society please quote your account number(s)

29. Give details of any present bank loans, hire purchase, maintenance or other commitments and state monthly payments.

*Delete as applicable.

PERSONAL DETAILS (CONTINUED)

Applicant Named in Question 1. **Applicant Named in Question 2.**

30. If you are a tenant, please enclose your rent book. If not available, please state the name and address of your landlord, and rent payable, and sign the enclosed Reference Form.

_____   _____

_____   _____

31. Are you at present an owner-occupier?   YES/NO*   YES/NO*

    If YES, please sign the enclosed Reference Form and state:

    Anticipated selling price   £ _____   £ _____

    If your present property is mortgaged or you have held a mortgage within the last two years, please state:

    Name and address of lender   _____   _____

    _____   _____

    A/c No. _____   A/c No. _____

    Repayment per month   £ _____   £ _____

    Approximate loan outstanding £ _____   £ _____

32. (a) How long have you been living
       at your present address?   _____ years   _____ years

    (b) How far are you moving?   _____ miles   _____ miles

33. Have you ever (i) been bankrupt or insolvent (ii) made any arrangement with your creditors (iii) had any judgment recorded against you (iv) executed any Bill of Sale?

    YES/NO* If YES, please supply details   YES/NO* If YES, please supply details

VALUATION AND SURVEY SERVICES

34. (a) **You will normally receive a copy of the Report and Valuation on the property** which is made by the Society's Valuer and intended solely for the consideration of the Society in determining what advance (if any) may be made on the security. The Report and Valuation is supplied for your own information and is not to be disclosed other than to your professional advisors. The inspection carried out is not a structural survey and there may be defects which a more detailed inspection would reveal. (See Declaration 35(a) below).

    (b) The Society's brochure on Valuation and Survey Services describes the **more detailed types of inspection** which can be undertaken by the Society's Valuer and sets out the fees you would pay.
    If you would like the Society to arrange a more detailed inspection please indicate which of the following reports you require:

    (i)   A Nationwide/RICS House Buyers Report (see Valuation and Survey Services brochure)   YES/NO*

    (ii) A full Structural Survey (see Valuation and Survey Services brochure)   YES/NO*

DECLARATION BY APPLICANT(S) (Please read carefully)

35. (a) I/We have read Paragraph 34 above and understand that no responsibility is implied or accepted by the Society or its Valuer for either the value or the condition of the property by reason of the Report and Valuation for mortgage purposes carried out on behalf of the Society by its Valuer.

    (b) I/We understand that the offer of or making of an advance will not imply any warranty that the purchase price of the property is reasonable.

    (c) I/We understand that borrowers are members of the Society and are bound by its Rules.

    (d) I/We acknowledge receipt of the current Mortgage Interest Rates and Valuation and Survey leaflets.

    (e) I/We agree that the Society may take up such reference it considers necessary and relevant to this mortgage application.

    (f) I/We declare the foregoing Statements and Particulars to be true and that the same shall form the basis of any arrangement for the advance (if any) made to me/us by the Society.

All applicants to sign here please

_____ Date _____

_____ Date _____

*Delete as applicable

Nationwide Building Society

M1 (8-85)

Inland Revenue
Relief for payment of loan interest at source

Lender's copy

To be completed by the lender

Name of lender _____ Branch office _____

Lender's reference _____
roll or loan number

A Amount of loan £ _____

If loan is a further advance -

Name(s) of borrower(s) _____

B New total outstanding £ _____

Address of property to _____
which the loan relates

To the borrower

Before you fill in this form, please read the notes overleaf. If you think you will be entitled to tax relief at source on your loan interest, please complete the form.

• Use a ball point pen. You do not need carbon paper.
• Read and sign the certificate below.
• Send **both** copies of the form back to your lender.

Please give
• the name of your Tax Office _____ your Tax Office reference number _____

• the name and address of your employer _____

_____

• or, if you are self-employed, your business address _____

For joint loans (husband and wife) information should relate to the husband

How the loan shown at A will be used

• Loan for house purchase *see Note 1* ... ... £ _____

• Loan to replace qualifying loan(s) on present property *see Note 1*

  1. Previous lender _____ Amount of loan replaced £ _____

    Purpose of original loan _____

  2. Previous lender _____ Amount of loan replaced £ _____

    Purpose of original loan _____
    (If more loans are being replaced, give details on a separate sheet and
    enter total of all such loans aside) ... ... £ _____

• Loan for home improvements - including further advances *see Note 5*
give precise details of the work, the date it was or will be carried out, and the cost - **receipts may be requested**

_____ £ _____

_____ £ _____

_____ £ _____

Total new loan £ _____
or further advance

Other loans
Give details of any other loan for which you get tax relief, but not loans being replaced or loans being added to by a further advance. If tax relief is given through 'MIRAS' tick the box 'MIRAS'

1. Lender _____ Amount of loan £ _____ ☐

2. Lender _____ Amount of loan £ _____ ☐

Certificate   *A false certificate can lead to prosecution*

I / We certify that -
• the whole of the new loan above has been or will be used in the way described for the purchase/improvement of my/our only/main residence *see Note 1*
• all other loans on my/our main residence for which I/we get tax relief have been shown above
• there is no exemption or immunity from tax on any part of my/our earnings or (in the case of a sole borrower) of the earnings of my wife or husband *see Note 6*
• the information I/we have given above is correct.

Signature(s) _____

Date _____
Loans taken out jointly by husband and wife - both must sign.
Loans in joint names (not husband and wife) - use separate forms. See Note 7

Miras 70

C

INSURANCE APPLICATION FORM

Before completing this Application Form please read the note on page 1 headed "DISCLOSURE OF FACTS WHICH MAY INFLUENCE AN INSURANCE PROPOSAL".

Will you occupy the property within 30 days of completion of the purchase?   YES/NO

If NO, will the property be fully furnished for habitation?   YES/NO

COMPLETE PART A **OR** B and return this form to your Branch Office with your mortgage application.

PART A.   "HOUSE & HOME" — COMBINED BUILDINGS AND CONTENTS INSURANCE

TO NATIONWIDE BUILDING SOCIETY

1.   I/We agree that, in the event of Nationwide Building Society granting me/us a mortgage, the insurance cover on the buildings and their contents be arranged under the Nationwide "House & Home" combined insurance scheme, with the Co-operative Insurance Society, unless the title deeds provide otherwise.

2.   I/We agree to pay the insurance premiums MONTHLY to Nationwide who will debit my/our account with the amount of the premiums as they fall due, and understand that any premiums remaining unpaid will bear interest.

☐   I/We also require accidental damage cover on buildings only.

NAME(S) _____   ALL APPLICANTS _____
BLOCK CAPITALS   TO SIGN

_____   _____

_____   _____

                                                                                DATE_____

PART B.   BUILDINGS INSURANCE ONLY

Complete this section only if you **do not** wish to arrange a "House & Home" policy.

TO NATIONWIDE BUILDING SOCIETY

1.   I/We agree that, in the event of Nationwide Building Society granting me/us a mortgage, the insurance cover on the buildings be arranged through the Co-operative Insurance Society, unless the title deeds provide otherwise.

2.   I/We agree that Nationwide will debit my/our account with the amount of the ANNUAL premiums as they fall due and, on my/our behalf, pay the premiums to the insurance company.

3.   I/We wish to be insured under Table 8.

☐   I/We also wish to include accidental damage cover on buildings only (Table 9).

NAME(S)_____   ALL APPLICANTS _____
BLOCK CAPITALS   TO SIGN

_____   _____

_____   _____

                                                                                DATE_____

I 73A (4-86)

You may well have been surprised by the amount of detail required by the building society. You should remember however:

a The society has a responsibility to its depositors (those who lend money to it). It must ensure that the borrower is capable of repaying the loan, and that the building against which the loan is secured is sound.

b The borrower is probably making his or her largest financial commitment ever, and so the building society must ensure that the commitment is not more than he or she can handle.

Activity 3	You should appreciate by now that the decision as to whether to rent or buy a house is not a simple one. Having discovered many aspects of the problem you should be able to describe it in terms easily understood by anyone. Write (or at least plan in note form) a magazine article aimed at young people about to get married and faced with the decision to rent or buy their house. The article should outline clearly the advantages and disadvantages of each possibility, and also advise them on the steps to be taken to research the decision in their area of the country.

Buying a house or flat

Your notes for Activity 3 should include some of the following observations:

Advantages

Chance of capital gain as value of house rises

Freedom to make alterations

Tax benefits on mortgage repayments

Eventual ownership of large capital asset

Pride in appearance and state of repair of own asset

Disadvantages

Large initial cost

Larger monthly payments

Repair and maintenance costs to bear

More difficult to move

Renting a house or flat

Advantages

Low initial cost
Smaller monthly repayments
Repairs and maintenance costs usually borne by landlord
Easier to move

Disadvantages

All payments are 'dead money' with no eventual capital asset
No chance to make alterations, and repairs may not be
    adequate
No tax benefits from borrowing
Loss of independence
No pride in appearance and state of repair of own asset

Activity 4	Many of the principles which you have discovered in relation to personal finance and the purchase or renting of a house are used in business. It has become much more common recently for businesses to hire or rent machinery and equipment rather than buy it outright. This activity requires you to examine the factors involved in such a decision.

Select a piece of business equipment, such as a
microcomputer, a photocopier, or a car. When you have
decided on a particular machine, or specification for a
machine, find out the following information about it:
a What is its cash purchase price?
b How much would it cost to obtain its use on some
    kind of contract hire for a given period of, say, two
    years?
c How much would it cost on Hire Purchase?
d How much would it cost if the money to buy the item
    were borrowed from the bank?

You should then write a short formal report, addressed
to your manager, outlining the factors to be taken into
account when obtaining your chosen piece of equipment.
The report should include a tabulation of relative costs
and, if possible, diagrams comparing the different
methods of financing the acquisition.

You would be well advised to concentrate your report on
three aspects of the problem:

a Firstly the businessman is always interested in the timing of payments, seeing it as preferable to delay payment wherever possible. The full reasons for this emerge in Block 9 on the purchase of a capital asset, and you may choose to use some of the techniques explained in that block to begin your solution to this problem. The discounted cash flow (DCF) method (see Block 9) becomes extremely complex when related to monthly payments however, and unless you have access to a computer package using this technique you are unlikely to perform a full DCF analysis on this problem. Nevertheless a general comment on the advantages of delaying or spreading payments should be included in your report, together with a tabulation and/or diagram to compare the methods.

b The overall cost of borrowing will also be of interest to the manager. If you pay cash there is no obvious cost of borrowing, but there is an opportunity cost of financing the asset. **Opportunity cost** means the cost of giving up another option by making a particular choice, and in this case it could be argued that the money used to buy the asset might have been invested in a deposit account to earn interest. If this were the case then the current rate of interest on an ordinary deposit account which gives the depositor reasonably quick access to his or her money should be included in your calculations when considering the cash purchase of the asset. In this way you will obtain a fairer comparison between the different methods of financing the asset.

c The third main aspect of your report should be to consider the benefits you are buying when hiring or renting an asset. Most hire or rental contracts provide for repair and servicing by the hirer. This should mean that, subject to the exact terms of the contract, breakdowns will not be costly and should be corrected quite quickly. On the other hand, if the asset has been purchased, the user takes the risk on repair costs. Most equipment of the type we are examining carries a guarantee of up to one year and so you may consider the risk worth taking for the second year. It is also possible in most cases to take out a service contract which covers all routine servicing and some repairs, and the cost of this must be added to the purchase price. This particular aspect of the problem is extremely difficult to quantify however, and most managers will have personal preferences for renting or buying which may outweigh the purely financial considerations.

Conclusion

In the field of personal finance, the purchase of a house or a flat is probably the most important financial decision you will make in your life. As a result of this, the research needed before committing yourself to such expenditure is considerable. This block has outlined the main factors which you should take into account when making the decision. It has also prepared you for the huge amount of detailed information which will be required by any financial institution lending you money.

In the same way a businessperson needing to buy a large fixed asset needs to show considerable caution so as not to make an unwise decision. Aspects of the way in which such an acquisition is to be financed will always be important to the well-being of the organization involved.

Block 3
Cash Control

Introduction

Throughout this book the word 'control' appears at various times. In a financial sense control is important. We all, as individuals, need to know what we earn and what we owe. Similarly businesses need this information, so that they can exercise some control over the movement of funds.

Most individuals do not keep 'accounts' in the formal way that businesses do, but they will have records of some sort to refer to so that they know at any one time what bills need to be paid, how much money is in the bank, and so on.

The amount of cash held in a bank needs to be monitored. If current accounts are overdrawn interest will be payable, so it is important to exercise careful control. Private individuals may, from time to time, need to arrange overdraft or loan facilities and interest will also be payable on these amounts.

Businesses keep formal cash and bill records, recording in the accounting system money received, detailing who has paid it in, and money paid out, similarly detailing to whom it was paid. Banks usually send out statements to customers detailing cash inflows and outflows. These need to be 'reconciled', (i.e. checked) by the account holder, so that the amount shown as the balance can be agreed.

Activity 1	On the next page is a bank statement for John and Mary Settle. It shows details of the money paid into their account and the money that is withdrawn. Banks produce these for customers regularly. This one gives the balance, at the top of the statement, of £156.46. It shows money withdrawn by cheque, standing order deductions for payments to a building society and an insurance company, and income paid in. A balance is shown after every transaction.

a What action do you think Mr and Mrs Settle will carry out when they receive this statement from the bank?

b Try to find out from your local banks or through other enquiries what some of the items in the statement mean, such as S.O. and DD. Then make sure that you understand the terms.

National Bank PLC   **Confidential**

Boreham branch   **Account**   **Sheet No**   199

Newtown   J & Mrs M Settle
                      10 Woodland Way
                      Branswood

Statement Date 2 Dec. 1986   **Account No** 01467924

Date	Details	Withdrawals	Deposits	Balance
1 Nov	Bal from sheet 198			156.46
2 Nov	000286	40.00		116.46
	Cash or chqs.		23.06	139.52
4 Nov	000287	38.94		
	000289	9.20		91.38
6 Nov	Newquay B/S S.O.	158.00		66.62 o/d
8 Nov	Cash or Chqs		136.00	69.38
10 Nov	Newtown 2 AC	40.00		29.38
15 Nov	Cash or Chqs.		136.00	165.38
18 Nov	000291	40.00		125.38
21 Nov	000292	30.00		95.38
26 Nov	CLM Insurance DD	24.00		71.38
27 Nov	Cash or Chqs		130.00	201.38

A bank statement for John and Mary Settle.

Assuming that the balance shown of £201.38 is correct, John and Mary Settle will have a record of what they have in their account. It will of course only be correct if all the transactions they have carried out are included. Sometimes cheques may not be presented to the bank in time for them to be included in statements. Similarly money may have gone in to the account that is not shown because of the date when the statement was produced.

A **reconciliation** will be necessary to adjust for these kind of occurrences, to make sure that the final balance figure is correct.

Cash control in businesses

For John and Mary Settle this reconciliation should be fairly simple. They do not have many transactions of income or expenditure. Businesses will have many transactions. They will also keep more detailed records than private individuals. Businesses need to know exactly how much money they owe to suppliers, and how much is owed to them by customers. Usually bank and cash records or 'accounts' will be kept by businesses, recording all payments and receipts. These records should show the same totals as the bank statement. Again, if there is a difference because of cheques not being presented or income not recorded, there is a need for a reconciliation to be completed to check the statement from the bank and to check the firm's records of income and expenditure.

We shall now move on to look at business situations where firms are keeping detailed records. When detailed records are kept it should be easier for a reconciliation to be achieved between the figures shown on the bank statement and those shown in the books of the company.

There will usually be differences however because of cheques not yet presented and so not appearing on the bank statement; this may be either for inflows (receipts) or outflows (payments) of cash.

| *Activity 2* | What would be the reconciled balance for a trader whose books show a balance of £83.50 in the bank on 24 April, but in addition: |

1 The trader has received cheques for £136.10, but he has not yet paid these into the bank.
2 £14.50 has been received by the trader, directly into his bank account, but so far he has not recorded these in his own accounts.
3 The trader has drawn cheques for £34.18, but these have not yet been presented at the bank.

Activity 2 will have shown how a reconciliation is necessary between the bank statement and the records kept by businesses. In large firms, where amounts involved are often massive, delays in recovering cash can be disastrous and a constant check needs to be kept.

Your answer to Activity 2 should show that the statement balance should be £3.92 overdrawn.

Good accounting practice would require you to lay out the statement proving this as follows:

Bank reconciliation statement at 24 April

	£	£
Balance as per cash book		83.50
Add Credit transfer not in cash book	14.50	
Unpresented cheques	34.18	48.68
		132.18
Less Cheques not yet banked		136.10
Balance as per bank statement		£3.92 overdrawn

Activity 3

This activity is more involved. You need to prepare a bank reconciliation statement, something like this:

Balance as shown in the accounts for bank balance	. . .
Adjust for amounts not yet paid into bank	. . .
Adjust for amounts not yet presented at bank	. . .
Balance as per bank statement	. . .

At the top of the next page is an extract from the records of Winterbottom Trading Company. As you can see the business is showing a balance at the bank of £536.72. The firm has recorded all the amounts coming in on the left of the account, the **debit** side and all the payments going out on the right-hand side, the **credit** side.

You need not concern yourself with the details of the accounting system but it is logical that any business would have to record the transactions it conducts in a fashion similar to this.

Date	Receipts		Date	Payments	chq No.	
May 1	BALANCE	616.94 *61694*	May 1	Purchases	86417	15.30 ✓
May 3	ABT Supplies	12.60	May 2	Avery PLC	86418	103.00 ✓
May 4	Cash receipts	102.91	May 2	Jones & Co	86419	210.15 ✓
May 8	FLW PLC	285.50	May 10	Petty cash	86420	21.11 ✓
May 10 ABC Ltd		*91.63*	May 11	JV & CO	86421	(3.20)
			May 14	Air flow PLC	86422	18.60 ✓
May 16	White PLC	102.11	May 16	Brown & Co.	86423	(125.00)
			May 18	Lee & Binks	86424	13.84 ✓
			May 21	Watkiss & Son	86425	265.20 ✓
May 25	Blue & Co	12.00	May 25	RCR Products	86426	(108.97)
			May 25	Grimaldi & Co	86427	11.00 ✓
May 29	Hamilton PLC	108.46	May 30	Petty cash	86428	(36.12)
May 30	Bryne & Sons	85.69	May 31	Balance		536.72 *535.72*
May 30	Coker & Day	36.12				
May 31	Clarke & Co	14.25				
		1468.21 *1467.21*				1468.21 *1467.21*

North East Bank PLC
Peterhead

Winterbottom Trading Company

Statement   Account No 0149443

Date			Debit	Credit	Balance
	Balance				625.21
May 3		86417	15.30 ✓		
		86419	210.15 ✓		
		86416	9.27 ✓		390.49
May 8	Cash/Cheques			401.01	791.50
May 16		86420	21.11 ✓		
		86422	18.60 ✓		
		86418	103.00 ✓		648.79
May 21	Cash/Cheques			193.74	842.53
May 22	FCT Insurance	SO	(25.00)		817.53
May 24		86424	13.84 ✓		
		86425	265.20 ✓		538.49
May 30	Cash/Cheques			206.15	744.64
May 31		86427	11.00 ✓		733.64
May 31	SM Agency	BGC		(19.00)	752.64

SO—Standing Order   CT Credit Transfer
DD—Direct Debit   BGC Bank Giro Credit

When the bank statement comes in from the firm's bank, the total should agree with the balance of £536.72. It probably will not, not necessarily because of errors, but because of delays in receipt or payment. On the previous page is shown the bank statement for you to reconcile with the amount shown in the records as the balance that should be in the bank.

Conclusion

As the business world becomes more complex, with methods of payment moving away from straight cash transactions, the activity of reconciling balances becomes more important and more involved.

We have looked in this block at the need to reconcile so that businesses and individuals can know precisely and exactly how much money they hold at any point in time. Large firms will not want large amounts of money 'lying' in a bank account. Money needs to work for individuals and businesses. It needs to earn a return, perhaps interest or dividends if invested in shares.

Knowing when to move money from a current account is important. This can best be done if business managers or individuals can be sure of the exact balance available at any point in time.

Block 4
Organizations, Finance and Measurement of Performance

Introduction

In the same way as an individual needs an income and spends money on a variety of items, an organization must obtain funds from somewhere in order to operate. Organizations may be classified in various ways and different types of organization will have different sources of funds and different uses for them. As a starting point for our study of the ways in which organizations manage their finances, we will examine three examples.

The High Street Motor Company

The High Street Motor Company is a small garage run by Harry Ford who operates as a sole trader. He is a 'one-man business', operating individually and having no partners. He repairs and services cars and trades in second-hand vehicles on a fairly small scale, usually having three or four cars to sell. He rents the building on a long-term lease, but has bought a lot of equipment and installed it himself.

The Meadowside Cricket and Football Club

The Meadowside Cricket and Football Club owns a ground just outside the town with a cricket square and football pitch on it. There is a small pavilion with changing rooms and the club also owns some sports equipment.

The Uphill Technical College

The Uphill Technical College is run by the County Council Education Committee in an old school building near the town centre. The college runs courses in Business Studies, Catering and Engineering and is well equipped for all the subject areas. Younger students attend the courses free but some students on adult and short courses are charged fees.

All these organizations have to obtain funds from somewhere in order to keep going. When they have obtained those funds they are either retained as cash or used to buy assets, which are items owned by the organization. Thus at any time the finances of the organization can be analysed in terms of where the finance has come from and what it has been used for.

| Activity 1 | For each of the three organizations above, you or your group should make two lists: |

a assets owned by the organization;
b sources of finance which might have paid for these assets.

The items which you have listed for Activity 1 should be typical of those which would normally appear on a **balance sheet**, a document which shows the current financial state of a business at any given time. The garage and the sports club would both prepare balance sheets at least once each year. The technical college, as part of the much wider organization of the education authority, is unlikely to analyse its finances in precisely the same way, but nevertheless such an analysis helps us to appreciate the basics.

One purpose of such a balance sheet is to help the owners and managers of the business or club to assess the security of the organization in financial terms. However, this can only really be done by comparing the positions of two or more organizations.

| Activity 2 | Harry Ford's Garage has one competitor in the town. The accounts for both firms are prepared by your employer, a chartered accountant, and on 31 December one year they had balances as shown at the top of the next page. |

a Draw up a balance sheet for each business. The layout for a balance sheet is explained on page 62. You will need to refer to the following section when attempting this activity.
b Decide which business appears to be in the stronger position. You may like to use some financial ratios to help you with your decision and examples of these are explained in the section on *Interpretation of accounts* (see page 74). However, such a technical approach is not

	Harry Ford	Norman Lang
	£	£
Second-hand cars for sale	6 350	8 530
Buildings	—	25 750
Sums owing by customers		
for service and repairs	850	1 580
Bills owing to suppliers		
of parts and materials	1 260	840
Equipment and tools at cost	6 000	4 000
Office equipment at cost	1 500	1 800
Depreciation to date		
Equipment and tools	1 350	1 330
Office equipment	610	550
Cash and bank		
Current account	360	(4 800) (overdrawn)
Mortgage loan	—	20 000
Bank 5-year loan	5 000	—

essential at this stage: common-sense comments about the figures would be quite adequate.

c On the evidence you have, to which business would you be more inclined to lend £6 000 for new computer diagnosis equipment? What other information would you need to make a more informed decision?

Balance sheets

A balance sheet is a document which shows the current financial state of an organization. The balance sheet includes three sections which are linked by an equation, a fixed piece of arithmetic, which means that the balance sheet will always balance because of the way in which each of its parts is defined. These parts are grouped into three categories.

Assets

Assets are items with a measurable financial value which are owned by an organization. Nowadays (see page 64) they appear on the left-hand side of the balance sheet, when using a horizontal presentation, and are normally separated into two main classes: **fixed assets** and **current assets**. Fixed assets are those items which the organization expects to keep for a long time to assist in its activities, such as buildings, vehicles and machinery. If it is not the normal business of the organization to trade in any of these items then it will usually buy such assets only occasionally and the purchase of such assets is known as **capital expenditure**. Those assets which are not fixed are known as current assets, and include cash, things which can quickly be turned into cash, or goods which have a relatively short life in the organization, usually less than a year.

Current assets for most organizations can be further divided into five categories:

a *Stock* Goods which the organization expects to sell or consume in the near future.

b *Debtors* The technical accounting term for amounts of money owed to an organization by outsiders and expected to be repayed within the coming year.

c *Prepayments* Payments in advance of expenses, the most common examples being local authority rates and insurance premiums, both of which are normally payable in advance of the provision of service.

d *Bank balances* Current accounts, or deposit accounts with a short period of call (ie money can be withdrawn from the account at reasonably short notice).

e *Cash* Notes and coins.

A distinction is usually drawn between the last two (bank balances and cash) in order to keep control over the way money is distributed between bank accounts and cash. Cash presents security problems in organizations and, where possible, it is usually better for money to be kept in bank accounts. You can find further information about this in Block 3.

Liabilities

Liabilities are amounts owed by an organization to outsiders. Nowadays liabilities are shown on the right-hand side of a balance sheet when using horizontal presentation. Liabilities may be unpaid bills from suppliers, unpaid bills for business expenses, or loans. Liabilities are defined as current if they are due for payment during the coming year. If they are not due for payment within the coming year, as might be the case with a bank loan or a mortgage, they are then classified as long-term liabilities and are shown in a separate section of the right-hand side of the balance sheet.

Capital

Capital represents the amount of money used to start a business or club only before the organization has undertaken any financial transactions. At all other times capital simply represents the difference between assets and liabilities. In the case of club accounts, capital is referred to as **accumulated fund**.

Another way to look at capital is that it is the amount owed by the organization to its owner or owners. If all the assets of the organization were turned into cash and the liabilities were all paid off, the remainder would be owed by the organization to its owner or owners.

The term **capital** is frequently used in different ways by businessmen and economists but to the accountant in the context of finance it is always the difference between assets and liabilities. If the amount of capital of an organization is not known, then it may be calculated by subtracting total liabilities from total assets.

Capital = Total assets *less* total liabilities

Should this result in a negative capital, ie if liabilities exceed assets, then the organization is insolvent and it is illegal for it to continue to trade when knowingly insolvent.

You should note that all the items in the balance sheet relate only to the business organization. The owner's personal belongings are not shown because the business is a separate entity and must be accounted for separately.

Sources of funds for organizations

Organizations acquire their funds from a number of sources, in the same way as individuals may have various sources of income and may also borrow money. If you are following a BTEC course you will study the various sources of funds for organizations in the double unit 'The Organization in its Environment'. Following is a series of definitions of sources of funds to enable you to interpret the accounts.

Share capital

Share capital is the general term applied to funds contributed by shareholders of a company, the shareholders thereby acquiring part ownership of the organization. There are a number of different types of share, the most common being **ordinary shares**. Ordinary share capital, sometimes referred to as **equity**, determines the overall ownership of the company although, in the case of a company having to close down, the ordinary shareholders are the last to be able to lay claim to the assets. Share capital is, therefore, the amount of funds originally contributed by the shareholders.

Loan capital

Loan capital is the name given to medium- or long-term loans made to a company. These may take the form of loans from banks or other financial institutions, or may be in the form of **debentures**. Debentures are individual loans of small amounts, usually units of £100, which are made by members of the public. Loan certificates are offered for sale by the company and a fixed rate of interest is paid against them. Possession of the loan certificates does not imply any ownership of the company.

Short-term funds

The company may gain the use of short-term funds through a bank overdraft or by buying goods on credit. Since such creditors will have to be paid within a normal accounting period, these funds appear as current liabilities in the balance sheet.

Information on sources of funds for clubs and for public organizations may be found elsewhere in this book (see Blocks 10 and 11), and a more detailed study of sources may be found in your study of 'The Organization in its Environment'.

Layout of the balance sheet

The following pages show the features of a simplified balance sheet. A similar document may be constructed for any organization by simply placing the assets and liabilities in the same positions on the balance sheet and if necessary calculating the capital.

There are various ways in which balance sheets may be displayed and the two most common methods are shown below for the same firm. The horizontal, or side-by-side, layout is often used when learning bookkeeping and accounts, whereas in practice the vertical layout is nearly always used.

Important note All balance sheets using the horizontal format in this book show assets on the left-hand side and liabilities on the right-hand side in accordance with the Companies Act 1981. You may find older examples with these positions reversed but this makes no difference to the essential meaning of the document. The convention of laying them out reversed is now being discontinued.

A balance sheet using a vertical layout for an organization operating as a sole trader.

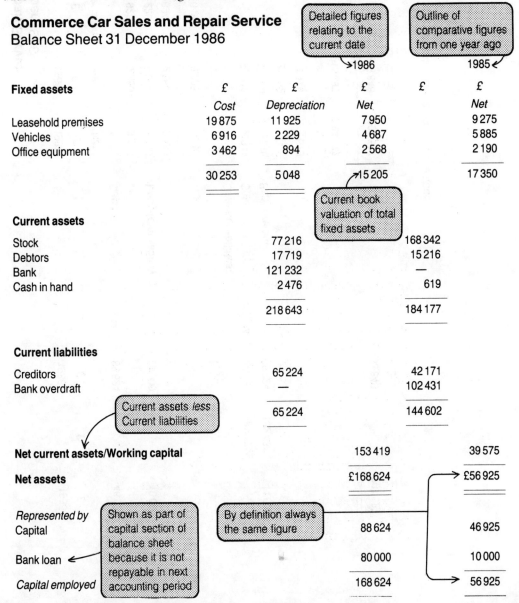

Commerce Car Sales and Repair Service
Balance Sheet 31 December 1986

Detailed figures relating to the current date

Outline of comparative figures from one year ago

Fixed assets	£	£	£	£	£
				1986	1985
	Cost	Depreciation	Net		Net
Leasehold premises	19 875	11 925	7 950		9 275
Vehicles	6 916	2 229	4 687		5 885
Office equipment	3 462	894	2 568		2 190
	30 253	5 048	15 205		17 350

Current book valuation of total fixed assets

Current assets					
Stock		77 216		168 342	
Debtors		17 719		15 216	
Bank		121 232		—	
Cash in hand		2 476		619	
		218 643		184 177	

Current liabilities					
Creditors		65 224		42 171	
Bank overdraft		—		102 431	
		65 224		144 602	

Current assets *less* Current liabilities

Net current assets/Working capital	153 419	39 575
Net assets	£168 624	£56 925

Shown as part of capital section of balance sheet because it is not repayable in next accounting period

By definition always the same figure

Represented by Capital	88 624	46 925
Bank loan	80 000	10 000
Capital employed	168 624	56 925

Commerce Car Sales and Repair Service
Balance Sheet as at 31 December 1986

Fixed assets	Cost	Depreciation	1986	1985
	£	£	Net £	Net £
Leasehold premises	19 875	11 925	7 950	9 275
Vehicles	6 916	2 229	4 687	5 885
Office equipment	3 462	894	2 568	2 190
	30 253	15 048	15 205	17 350

Current assets		
Stock	77 216	168 342
Debtors	77 219	15 216
Bank	121 232	—
Cash in hand	2 476	619
	218 643	184 177
	233 848	201 527

	1986		1985	
	£	£	£	£
Capital		88 624		46 925
Long-term liability		80 000		10 000
Current liabilities				
Creditors	65 224		42 171	
Bank overdraft	—	65 224	102 431	144 602
		233 848		201 527

A balance sheet using a horizontal layout for an organization operating as a sole trader.

Level of activity in an organization

You probably came to the conclusion in Activity 2 that you needed to know something about the amount of work each business was doing as well as what it owned in order to be able to judge its potential and reliability. A balance sheet only shows the position at a moment in time and consequently any business or other organization must keep records of their activities between the times when balance sheets are produced. Many organizations use a system of record keeping called double-entry bookkeeping, which is a self-checking system of recording all financial activities during the accounting period. The details of this system are outside of the scope of this course, but at the end of each accounting period a summary of all the activities is extracted from those records and presented in the form of a **Trading and Profit and Loss Account** in the case of businesses, and a **Trading and Income and Expenditure Account** in the case of non-profit making organizations, such as clubs or societies. These accounts record details of revenue expenditure and details of non-cash expenses, such as depreciation and bad debts, while any capital expenditure simply involves a change in the figures shown in the balance sheet.

| *Activity 3* | The following figures give details of trading and expenses for the two garages in Activity 2 in the same year as the balance sheets which you have already constructed: |

	Harry Ford	Norman Lang
	£	£
Sales of cars and work done	60 500	76 200
Purchases of cars and materials	44 200	55 890
Stock of cars and parts at 1 Jan.	4 530	6 370
Interest charges	680	2 970
Wages of only employee	4 680	5 130
Rates	390	475
Insurance	180	240
Machinery maintenance	1 650	1 950
Sundry expenses	585	480
Electricity and heating	1 260	1 475
Depreciation for the year		
Equipment and tools	900	600
Office equipment	225	55

a Draw up a trading and profit and loss account for each firm. There is an example of how to do this below and you will find that you need to refer to this when attempting this activity.

b Which of the two firms appears to be doing better? Does this change your mind about the judgement you made in Activity 2? You may choose to use some financial ratios to support your case. Write a letter to each client advising them on the likelihood of their obtaining a loan. Advice on interpretation of accounts is given below.

c In each case the proprietor of the firm could earn about £6000 a year as a mechanic if he could work for somebody else. List all the factors he should take into account when deciding whether to stay in business.

Trading and profit and loss accounts

In addition to showing its current financial position in the balance sheet, a firm also needs to summarize the flow of income and expenditure for each trading period, mainly in order to calculate its profits. This calculation is performed in the trading and profit and loss account using a conventional layout which always shows certain items.

The two types of profit calculated by most firms are **gross profit** and **net profit**.

Gross profit = Sales revenue *less* **Cost of goods sold**

Net profit = Gross profit *less* **Business expenses**

Sales revenue

Sales revenue is the value of all goods or services sold during the period in question. This is not normally equal to receipts of cash as it includes goods or services sold on credit and not yet paid for. The position relating to amounts owing is shown in the balance sheet. A credit sale is normally taken as having occurred when the customer is invoiced.

Cost of sales

Cost of sales (*or* cost of goods sold) is calculated by taking the value of goods purchased during the period and adjusting it to allow for stock held at the start and end of the period. As with sales revenue, a purchase on credit is taken to have been made when invoiced and not when paid for.

The example on page 68 shows the way in which the calculation of the cost of sales is included in the trading account.

Stock

Stock is valued at **cost** or **market value**, whichever is the lower. This is in accordance with the accountancy convention of *prudence*, ensuring that an organization does not overstate the value of the assets which it holds. The stock held at the beginning of an accounting period is usually known as the **opening stock** and that held at the end of the accounting period is known as the **closing stock**.

Gross profit

Gross profit, the difference between sales revenue and cost of goods sold, measures the amount by which a trader marks up his goods before selling them. The amount of gross profit made compared with the volume of business done is an important measure of the style of trading chosen by a businessman and the accounting ratios relating to this are important measures of business performance.

Later in this block we shall examine ways of assessing and comparing the performance of business organizations. This is done by using percentages and other relative measures known as **accounting ratios**. Some of these reveal the style of trading operated by an organization by comparing sales revenue, cost of goods sold, and gross profit.

Business expenses

Business expenses are those costs which the business has to bear other than the direct cost of the goods. They are sometimes referred to as overheads and common examples of them are shown in the profit and loss account on the next page. They include depreciation, which is a charge against which the asset is purchased. A complete examination of depreciation will be made later in this block.

Net profit

Net profit measures the remaining income for an organization after all costs have been taken into account. It is generally the figure on which the firm's tax liability is calculated and, like the measurements of gross profit, the accounting ratios involving net profit are most important measures of business performance.

A version of the trading and profit and loss account which is designed to give information to help the managers of the firm, and which includes certain ratios and comparative statistics, is known as an **operating statement**.

Commerce Car Sales and Repair Service
Profit and Loss Account for the year ended 31 December 1986

	Figures for the current period £	1986 £	£	1985 £
Sales/Turnover			527 200	482 190
Opening stock	168 342		199 000	Figures for the accounting period for comparison
Add Purchases	325 895		345 848	
	494 237		544 848	
Less Closing stock	77 216		168 342	
Cost of sales		417 021		376 506
Gross profit		110 179		105 684
Expenses				
Wages and salaries	55 504		59 417	
Rent and rates	13 800		12 000	
Heat and light	1 702		1 621	
Repairs and renewals	501		429	
Insurance	2 000		2 500	
Advertising, printing and stationery	3 000		1 853	
Telephone and postage	1 177		1 121	
Interest on bank loan	8 250		2 200	
Audit and accountancy fee	1 500		1 200	
Motor vehicle expenses	1 000		1 575	
Sundry expenses	725		691	
Depreciation	3 234	92 393	3 560	88 167
Net profit for year		**£17 786**		**£17 517**

Annotations (callout boxes):
- Sales *less* Cost of sales → **Gross profit**
- Gross profit *less* Total expenses → **Net profit for year**

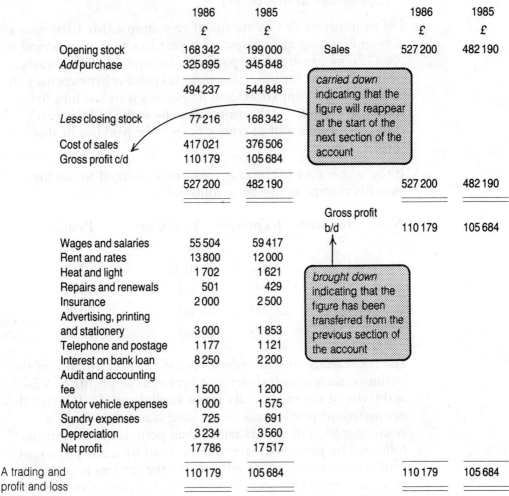

Commerce Car Sales and Repair Service
Trading and Profit and Loss Account for the year ended
31 December 1986

	1986 £	1985 £		1986 £	1985 £
Opening stock	168 342	199 000	Sales	527 200	482 190
Add purchase	325 895	345 848			
	494 237	544 848	*carried down indicating that the figure will reappear at the start of the next section of the account*		
Less closing stock	77 216	168 342			
Cost of sales	417 021	376 506			
Gross profit c/d	110 179	105 684			
	527 200	482 190		527 200	482 190
			Gross profit b/d	110 179	105 684
Wages and salaries	55 504	59 417			
Rent and rates	13 800	12 000			
Heat and light	1 702	1 621	*brought down indicating that the figure has been transferred from the previous section of the account*		
Repairs and renewals	501	429			
Insurance	2 000	2 500			
Advertising, printing and stationery	3 000	1 853			
Telephone and postage	1 177	1 121			
Interest on bank loan	8 250	2 200			
Audit and accounting fee	1 500	1 200			
Motor vehicle expenses	1 000	1 575			
Sundry expenses	725	691			
Depreciation	3 234	3 560			
Net profit	17 786	17 517			
	110 179	105 684		110 179	105 684

A trading and profit and loss account using a horizontal layout.

Depreciation

You have already discovered that fixed assets are subject to depreciation. In order for you to understand the construction of final accounts fully, a fairly lengthy explanation of this term is now needed.

A fixed asset should last for more than one accounting period. When a fixed asset is bought by an organization there are two reasons why its cost should not all be charged against the profits for that period:

(Left) A trading and profit and loss account using a vertical layout.

a because the asset still has a value at the end of the period and this value should be reflected in the accounts, *b* because if the purchase of several fixed assets were charged to the period in which they were bought, profits would fluctuate wildly according to the amount of capital expenditure in that period.

Let us illustrate this by means of an example. Mr Park runs a taxi and his average receipts each year in a four-year period are £12600. From this he pays out, on average, £2600 each year for petrol, repairs, insurance, tax, and other expenses. A new taxi costs him £8000 and he expects it to last him for four years. How much 'profit' does he make in each year? (His own wages will of course have to be paid out of this 'profit'.)

If the whole cost of the taxi were to be charged to the first year his profits would be as follows:

Year	Income £	Expenses £	Taxi Cost £	Profit £
1	12600	2600	8000	2000
2	12600	2600	nil	10000
3	12600	2600	nil	10000
4	12600	2600	nil	10000

For tax reasons, and in order to judge the performance of the business, such a wide difference between the profits in Year 1 and those of the other years is not at all desirable. In general, organizations pay less tax in the long run if they show a consistent level of profits rather than periods of high profits followed by periods of large losses. If an irregular pattern of profits occurs, it is more difficult for the owners to judge the performance of the firm. If, however, the cost of the taxi is spread over the four years, the results would be as follows:

Year	Income £	Expenses £	Depreciation £	Profit £
1	12600	2600	2000	8000
2	12600	2600	2000	8000
3	12600	2600	2000	8000
4	12600	2600	2000	8000

This pattern of profits would reflect more accurately the steady nature of the business during the period in question.

The type of depreciation used in the above example is known as **straight-line** or **equal instalment** depreciation and simply involves spreading the cost equally over the expected life of the asset. The book or accounting value of the asset at any time is found by subtracting the total depreciation charged to date from the original cost of the asset. Hence the value of the taxi to be shown on Mr Park's balance sheet at the end of Year 3 would be

$$£8000 - (£2000 \times 3 \text{ years}) = £2000.$$

If this is related to the second-hand car market, one can see that this method is unlikely to reflect the current value of the vehicle. The balance sheet value of the asset will therefore not necessarily reflect the market value of any asset.

An alternative method of charging depreciation which sometimes reflects the fall in value of fixed assets more precisely is known as the **reducing balance method**. Using this method a fixed proportion of the remaining value of the asset is charged as depreciation in each year. If this method were applied to our example using a rate of 30% per annum, depreciation would be calculated as follows:

	£
Cost of taxi	8 000
Year 1 depreciation (30% of £8000)	2 400
Book value at the end of year 1	5 600
Year 2 depreciation (30% of £5600)	1 680
Book value at the end of year 2	3 920
Year 3 depreciation (30% of £3920)	1 176
Book value at the end of year 3	2 744
Year 4 depreciation (30% of £2744)	823
Book value at the end of year 4	1 921

Using this method therefore the book value of the asset is never reduced to zero!

The **book value** of an asset is the original cost less the total depreciation written off to date.

Book value = Cost of asset *less* Depreciation to date

The result of using this method with respect to Mr Park's profits is as follows:

Year	Income	Expenses	Depreciation	Profit
		£	£	£
1	12 600	2 600	2 400	7 600
2	12 600	2 600	1 680	8 320
3	12 600	2 600	1 176	8 824
4	12 600	2 600	823	9 177

Thus the pattern of reported profits produced by this method is different again. An important feature of depreciation is that the method chosen by the management of an organization can affect the level of reported profits, so the accounting convention of consistency should be applied to ensure that changes are not made simply to change the pattern of reported profits.

With some major assets, such as buildings, neither of the above methods is used but a system of **periodic revaluation** is applied.

The value of land and buildings tends to rise rather than fall over time. An organization may feel that the balance sheet value of such assets is so out of line with current market values that it distorts the true and fair view which the accounts should present. These assets may then be revalued by a professional valuer. The increase does not count as profit but simply becomes part of the capital section of the balance sheet.

The sets of accounts on the opposite page show the effect of revaluation. The land and buildings are revalued on 1 January 1986 and the professional valuer estimates that they are worth at least £52 000.

Sets of accounts
showing the effect
of revaluation.

Abridged balance sheet of D. Stevenson as at 31 December 1985

	£	£
Fixed Assets		
Land and buildings		35 000
Vehicles		15 000
		50 000
Current assets	7 800	
Less current liabilities	4 300	
Working capital		3 500
Net assets		£53 500
Represented by		
Capital		34 500
Mortgage loan		19 000
Capital employed		£53 500

Abridged balance sheet of D. Stevenson as at 1 January 1986

	£	£
Fixed Assets		
Land and buildings		52 000
Vehicles		15 000
		67 000
Current assets	7 800	
Less current liabilities	4 300	
Working capital		3 500
Net assets		£70 500
Represented by		
Capital		51 500
Mortgage loan		19 000
Capital employed		£70 500

Interpretation of final accounts

As well as the legal requirement to keep good books of account for tax purposes, a businessperson will wish to use his or her accounts to monitor the progress of the business. By reading the signs in the figures carefully the owner of a business can make more considered judgements and decisions about the future conduct of the business. In order to understand the ways in which accounts may be interpreted we will examine the final accounts of two businesses in the same industry and compare their performances. You should be careful when interpreting accounts to ensure that differences between businesses actually relate to their efficiency and performance. If they are in different industries, different places, or are very different in size, then your interpretation of the financial statements should take this into account.

Shown opposite are the final accounts for two businesses in the retail food trade.

The Supasell Supermarket is a small self-service store in a residential area dealing in a wide range of fairly cheap food. It carries a limited variety of stock covering the basic range of food and household items.

The Refined Foods Shop is a small exclusive shop which specializes in exotic foods near the middle of a town. It carries a huge variety of goods and both the exotic foods and the basic items which it does sell are quite expensive.

When interpreting final accounts we are interested in three features:
a **Profitability**   the extent to which the business is making a profit appropriate to its size and industry,
b **Liquidity**   the ability of a business to cover its debts as and when required,
c **Use of assets** or **activity measures**   the way in which the amount of assets employed in the business compares with the activity generated by the business.

We shall first see how each ratio is calculated and then examine the interpretation of both sets of accounts.

Supasell Supermarket

Trading and profit and loss account for year ended 31 December 1986

	1986	1985
	£	£
Sales	280 000	238 000
Opening stock	14 300	13 900
Add purchases	248 600	213 500
	262 900	227 400
Less closing stock	14 680	14 300
Cost of goods sold	248 220	213 100
Gross profit	31 780	24 900
Less expenses		
Wages	10 800	8 900
Rates, insurance	700	650
Electricity	680	610
Interest	3 700	3 900
Other expenses	900	900
	16 780	15 000
Net profit	£15 000	£9 900

Balance sheet as at 31 December 1986

	1986	1985
	£	£
Fixed assets		
Buildings and fixtures	80 000	80 000
Vehicles	8 000	3 000
	88 000	83 000
Current assets		
Stock	14 680	14 300
Debtors	1 320	590
Cash	200	310
	16 200	15 200
Current liabilities		
Creditors	4 100	3 700
Tax owing	2 200	2 000
Bank overdraft	2 100	2 800
	8 400	8 500
Net current assets	7 800	6 700
	£95 800	£89 700
Financed by		
Capital	60 800	54 700
Mortgage loan	35 000	35 000
	£95 800	£89 700

Final accounts for Supasell Supermarket.

Refined Foods

Trading and profit and loss account for year ended 31 December 1985				Balance sheet as at 31 December 1986		

Trading and profit and loss account for year ended 31 December 1985

	1986	1985
	£	£
Sales	127 100	123 100
Opening stock	13 800	13 900
Add purchases	100 300	94 700
	114 100	108 600
Less closing stock	13 700	13 800
Cost of goods sold	100 400	94 800
Gross profit	26 700	28 300
Less expenses		
Wages	6 200	5 600
Rent, Rates, Insurance	4 790	4 750
Electricity	570	540
Interest	1 070	990
Other expenses	470	520
	13 100	12 400
Net profit	£13 600	£15 900

Balance sheet as at 31 December 1986

	1986	1985
	£	£
Fixed assets		
Fixtures	4 800	3 900
Vehicles	7 000	8 000
	11 800	11 900
Current assets		
Stock	13 700	13 800
Debtors	4 200	3 700
Bank and cash	1 600	1 200
	19 500	18 700
Current liabilities		
Creditors	2 300	3 100
Tax owing	3 200	3 600
	5 500	6 700
Net current assets	14 000	12 000
	£25 800	£23 900
Financed by		
Capital	17 800	15 900
5-year bank loan repayable 1989	8 000	8 000
	£25 800	£23 900

Final accounts for Refined Foods.

Profitability

We shall examine three ways of measuring the profitability of a business.

a Gross profit as a percentage of sales

This ratio, which is sometimes known as the **margin**, is calculated as

$$\textbf{Gross profit as a percentage of sales} = \frac{\textbf{Gross profit} \times \textbf{100}}{\textbf{Sales}}.$$

For Supasell Supermarket for 1986 the calculation would be

$$\frac{£31\,780 \times 100}{£280\,000} = 11.35\%.$$

This ratio indicates the percentage by which a trader has been able to increase the cost price of the goods before selling them. If the gross profit is expressed as a percentage of the cost of goods sold this is known as the **mark-up**, whereas if it is expressed as a percentage of sales it is known as the **margin**. Either ratio may be used when making comparisons between businesses or when monitoring the performance of a business through successive accounting periods. A firm may choose to set its prices at a level which produces a lower percentage in order to attract more sales, so the ratio should not be taken as a measure of efficiency. When read in conjunction with the activity ratio called the **rate of stock turnover** (see *Activity indicators* below) it will indicate the style of trading adopted by the firm (high volume/low margin or low volume/high margin).

b Net profit as a percentage of sales

$$\textbf{Net profit as a percentage of sales} = \frac{\textbf{Net profit} \times \textbf{100}}{\textbf{Sales}}.$$

For Supasell Supermarket for 1986 the calculation would be

$$\frac{£15\,000 \times 100}{£280\,000} = 5.36\%.$$

This ratio depends largely on the type of industry in which the firm is operating. It is therefore advisable to compare it only with similar firms or with the same ratio in the same firm for a different accounting period.

c Net profit as a percentage of capital employed

$$\textbf{Net profit as a percentage} \atop \textbf{of capital employed} = \frac{\textbf{Net profit} \times \textbf{100}}{\textbf{Capital empoyed}}$$

For Supasell Supermarket for 1986 the calculation would be

$$\frac{£15\,000 \times 100}{£95\,800} = 15.66\%.$$

Because it is the only figure available, we have used the end of year *capital employed* figure shown in the balance sheet. If available, a start of year figure or an average should be used as the profits earned during the year and included in our end of year figure are not being used by the business for the whole of the year.

This ratio represents the equivalent of the interest being earned on the funds invested in the organization. It should therefore compare favourably with the percentage interest which would be earned if the funds were placed in a secure investment elsewhere, bearing in mind that the owner may well be taking an additional risk by being in business. The ratio should therefore be higher than the current bank rate in order to stop the businessman from moving onto safer ground. A ratio which is lower than the bank rate is unlikely to be tolerated for very long by the investor in the firm. This ratio is often referred to as the **return on capital employed**.

The profitability ratios for the other accounts relating to Supasell Supermarket and Refined Foods are shown in the table on page 81.

d Analysis of expenses

In the accounts for Refined Foods and Supasell Supermarkets, each of the items of expense, such as wages, rates, or insurance, could be shown as a percentage of either sales or cost of sales to give some measure of comparability between different accounting periods and also between different businesses.

Liquidity

Liquidity, or the availability of cash or near–cash to pay debts, is measured in two main ways.

a The current ratio

This ratio compares current assets with current liabilities:

$$\textbf{Current ratio} = \frac{\textbf{Current assets}}{\textbf{Current liabilities}} : \textbf{1}$$

For Supasell Supermarket for 1986 the calculation would be

$$\frac{£16\,200}{£8\,400} = 1.93:1.$$

Although the value of this ratio may vary between industries, and between firms in different stages of development, a general guideline would be that it should be about 2:1. If it is significantly smaller than this the firm may have trouble in meeting its liabilities at short notice. If it is significantly higher than this it may indicate that the firm has funds tied up in stock, amounts owed to it by debtors, or ready cash available, which is not being used to full advantage.

Clearly Supasell has this ratio at what is regarded as a satisfactory level at the end of 1986. As a measure of liquidity on its own however, this ratio can be misleading and the management of Supasell would be well advised to look at the next indicator of liquidity!

b The liquid assets or acid test ratio

This ratio compares liquid assets with current liabilities:

$$\textbf{Liquid assets} = \frac{\textbf{Current assets less stock}}{\textbf{Current liabilities}} : \textbf{1}$$

For Supasell Supermarket for 1986 the calculation would be

$$\frac{£16\,200 - 14\,680}{£8\,400} = 0.18:1.$$

Since this ratio measures the funds available in cash or near-cash to pay debts which may become due in the near future, Supasell's position looks less healthy now. As a general rule the ratio should be about 1:1 so that any sudden call on funds can be met, and if it is significantly below this the firm must have quick access to other funds if it is not to be vulnerable to bankruptcy proceedings. Should the ratio be too much in excess of 1:1, the firm is not making best use of its funds and should reconsider its policy.

Activity indicators

Organizations may work at a slow pace or a fast pace. They may make full use of their resources or they may simply 'tick over', being happy to continue in existence without being overambitious.

To measure the level of activity one must take note of a number of factors, but within any given industry and style of business two measures may be effectively used.

a Sales to capital employed

This ratio relates the amount of business transacted by an organization to the amount of funds invested in it:

$$\textbf{Sales to capital employed} = \frac{\textbf{Sales}}{\textbf{Capital employed}}$$

For Supasell Supermarket for 1986 the calculation would be

$$\frac{£280\,000}{£95\,800} = 2.92.$$

There is no set level for this ratio but an organization often monitors changes in it to establish whether it is making effective use of its resources. Changes in this ratio from one accounting period to another are far more significant than any comparison with the ratios of other organizations. The value of the ratio will also be affected by the decisions of management relating to the rent or purchase of fixed assets in that it is much easier to achieve a high ratio if assets are rented rather than purchased.

b The rate of stock turnover (the stockturn ratio)

This ratio establishes a relationship between the level of stock held and the volume of business transacted during the accounting period:

$$\textbf{Rate of stock turnover} = \frac{\textbf{Cost of goods sold}}{\textbf{Average stock}} \quad \textbf{times per accounting period}$$

For Supasell Supermarket for 1986 the calculation would be

$$\frac{£248\,220}{£14\,490} = 17.1 \text{ times.}$$

The value of this ratio is expressed as a 'number of times' since it indicates the extent to which sales represent the complete clearing of the shelves in a year. Any business holding stock will wish to achieve as high a rate of stock turnover as possible.

The average stock for the calculation of this ratio is taken to be the arithmetic mean of the most detailed sets of stock figures available. In most cases this is found by taking a simple arithmetic mean of the opening stock and the closing stock.

The rate of stock turnover, when examined together with the gross profit to sales percentage, will indicate a style of trading. A firm may aim for high turnover and low margin, or low turnover and high margin, to achieve the same effect. Clearly, our example of Supasell and Refined Foods shows two contrasting styles of trading and for each firm the main interest of the ratios would be to compare their performance between one accounting period and another.

Interpretation of a group of ratios

The table below shows a set of ratios calculated from final accounts for the years 1985 and 1986:

	Supasell Supermarket		Refined Foods	
	1986	1985	1986	1985
Gross profit as a percentage of sales	11.35%	10.46%	21.01%	22.99%
Net profit as a percentage of sales	5.36%	4.16%	10.70%	12.92%
Net profit as a percentage of capital employed	15.66%	11.04%	52.71%	66.53%
Sales : Capital employed	2.92	2.65	4.93	5.15
Rates of stock turnover	17.1	15.1	7.3	6.8
Current ratio	1.93:1	1.79:1	3.55:1	2.79:1
Liquid assets (or acid test ratio)	0.18:1	0.11:1	1.05:1	0.73:1
Expenses as a percentage of total				
Wages	64.4	59.3	47.3	45.1
Rates etc.	4.2	4.3	36.6	38.3
Electricity	4.0	4.1	4.4	4.4
Loan interest	22.0	26.0	8.2	8.0
Other expenses	5.4	6.3	3.5	4.2

When comparing the situation and performance of the two organizations using the above information, and the interpretation of each ratio as outlined above, the following points should be made and should be incorporated into any report comparing the two.

Profitability

a During the two years in question Supasell has been able to increase its margin while Refined Foods has reduced its margin.

b Supasell has shown efficiency in increasing its net profit as a percentage of sales ratio, but Refined Foods, though deteriorating, is still achieving a much higher ratio.

c The return on capital employed is much higher for Refined Foods largely because the premises are rented, so the capital employed is much lower.

d Supasell is improving its return on capital employed while Refined Foods' ratio is declining.

e The Refined Foods return on capital employed is very high compared with normal levels of interest on investments but should be regarded with caution when read together with the liquidity ratios.

Liquidity

a In terms of the current ratio both firms have strengthened their positions. Supasell has a ratio near to the rule-of-thumb recommended level but should beware of taking comfort from this single indicator. Refined Foods has increased its ratio to a point where one must question whether it is making best use of its resources.

b The liquid assets ratio indicates a totally different picture for Supasell Supermarkets. The level of the ratio must mean that should the creditors demand rapid repayment of their debts the firm would be placed in a very difficult position.

c The situation of Supasell Supermarket may be explained by the security of its fixed assets in the form of buildings, which may in turn lead to extensive guarantees from the bank to increase its overdraft to an appropriate level to cover any imminent demands.

d Refined Foods appears to be in a stable situation with regard to its ability to meet any sudden call on funds.

Measures of activity

a As one might expect from their names, and the brief descriptions of the firms, Refined Foods operates on a low turnover/high margin style of trading while Supasell Supermarket operates on a high turnover/low margin style.

b Both firms have successfully increased their rate of stock turnover over the two years in question.

c While Supasell Supermarket has improved the use of its assets as indicated by the Sales/Capital employed ratio, that of Refined Foods has declined.

d Both firms have increased their sales turnover but Supasell has achieved the higher rate of increase.

Analysis of expenses

a As one would expect, Supasell with the owned premises, and the mortgage, pays higher interest charges and lower property expenses (rent, rates, insurance, etc.).

b Wages have risen proportionally in both organizations but more so in Supasell.

These percentages would be of use to both organizations in monitoring changes in spending patterns during successive accounting periods.

General

The above are just some of the points revealed by the accounts. To make more judgements on the performance of the firms would require more detailed figures and more detailed knowledge of the other aspects of the organization. The interpretation of accounts is a complex matter and care must be taken, especially over two points:

a **Don't** read more into the figures than is really there without additional information and knowledge about the firm and its activities.

b **Don't** draw conclusions from a single ratio without taking into account comparisons with other similar accounts and the other ratios in the firm's own accounts.

On the next page is a summary of the procedure for interpreting accounting statements which can be used as an initial general guide.

Summary of procedure for interpreting accounting statements

Calculate ratios under the following headings:

1 *Profitability*
   Gross profit as a percentage of sales
   Net profit as a percentage of sales
   Net profit as a percentage of capital employed

2 *Liquidity*
   Current ratio
   Acid test ratio

3 *Activity*
   Sales : Capital employed
   Rate of stock turnover

4 *Expenses analysis*
   Individual expenses as a percentage of total expenses

Tabulate ratios, with comparative figures from other organizations or from previous periods.

Draw conclusions from differences shown in tabulated figures, either differences from normal values or changes from previous periods.

Activity 4

Following earlier activities and the practice here in preparing and interpreting a simple set of final accounts, you should now be in a position to carry out the following activity. If possible, work with a small group of people to plan the setting up of a business. Your plan should ultimately be in the form of a proposal to a bank manager from whom you are seeking a loan to start the business. The following steps are suggested before you attempt to write the final proposal to the bank manager:

a Select a type of business which you feel might be successful in your area.

b Take advice to make a reasonable estimate of the volume of business you feel you may be able to generate in the first year.

c Investigate the likely costs involved in the business, including the cost of interest on the money borrowed. Your estimates of these costs should be based on research of prices in your area.

d Prepare a set of estimated final accounts for the first year (these would be known as **budgeted accounts** as

they are only a plan of what you expect to happen).
e Write a report to the bank manager requesting the loan
and giving details of all your estimates.
If it is at all possible your report should be shown to a
bank manager, or other person in a position to grant
loans, so that he or she can comment on it and suggest
ways in which it might be improved.

Budgets and budgeting

A budget is a financial plan for a future period of time. It is
normally prepared in the form of a set of final accounts
summarizing a more detailed set of figures which list all the
types of income and expenditure for the organization in order
to form a plan of what should occur under each heading. A
budget is not necessarily the same as a forecast of what is
expected to happen, as it may be used to set targets at which
each section of the organization should aim. Budgetary
control is achieved by management ensuring that limits to
spending as set by the budget are observed, and the overall
performance of various parts of the organization is measured
by comparing actual figures with budgets. Budgets are
particularly important in public sector organizations as a
control on spending. 'A budget' is the name given to the
overall plan for the organization, but each account may be
referred to separately as a budgeted account, and a separate
plan called a 'cash budget' is usually prepared to show plans
for liquid funds (assets which are either in the form of cash or
some other readily usable medium of exchange) passing
through the organization during the period.

Club accounts

Activity 5 | Obtain the accounts of two or three clubs or societies.
These are not usually highly confidential and many clubs
issue a copy to members at the Annual General Meeting
each year. Study these accounts, select one set, and
prepare a written or oral report which you can make,
acting as treasurer of the club or society and reporting to
members. Your report should include a statement of the
current position as revealed in the balance sheet, the

significant events of the year as revealed in the bank account or income and expenditure account, and any suggestions you might have as a new treasurer to improve the quality of information in the accounts. Your report should be suitably illustrated with charts or diagrams to reinforce the main points you are making.

A club or non-profit making society usually keeps accounts and reports to members in much the same way as a firm reports to its shareholders or prepares accounts for tax purposes. The end-of-year accounts for a club or society are very similar to the final accounts of a firm and include a balance sheet (although this is sometimes called a **statement of affairs**) and a profit and loss account (although this is usually known as an **income and expenditure account**). If a club runs a trading operation, such as a bar, then a trading account is prepared in the same way as for a commercial firm. Subscriptions from members are treated as an item of income and appear in the income and expenditure account for the year of membership which has been paid, regardless of when the treasurer receives the money. Members of the club may therefore also be debtors if they are behind with their payments of subscriptions, or creditors if they have paid in advance. Another item which may occur on the income side of the income and expenditure account is the profit on an event or function (a loss would of course appear on the expenditure side). Rather than showing all the details of each function during the year, the profit on each event is usually worked out separately and a single figure shown in the income and expenditure account.

More details of club accounts are examined in Block 10.

The parallels between accounts of clubs and societies and those of business organizations are summarized in the table below.

Business organizations	**Clubs or societies**
Trading account	Trading account for a specific trading operation e.g. a bar or shop
Cash account	Receipts and payments account

Profit and loss account calculating net profit	Income and expenditure account showing surplus or deficit

Net profit = Gross profit *less* expenses

	Gross profit on trading
Add	Subscriptions for year
	Profits on specific events
	Other incomes
Less	Losses on specific events
Less	Expenses
	= Surplus or deficit

Balance sheet	Balance sheet or Statement of affairs

Activity 6

Case study: The Southern Cross Athletic Club
The accounts for the Southern Cross Athletic Club are shown on the following pages. It is not normally appropriate to calculate ratios or to interpret club accounts in the same way as those of commercial organizations. The club treasurer however has to face the members at the annual general meeting in order to present a brief report and answer questions.
  a Write notes for the treasurer on the main points revealed by the accounts which he should include in his report.
  b Make a list of questions which he might anticipate from members.

Guidance on Activity 6

As club treasurer you might choose to mention any of the following interesting points which appear in the accounts. Those which you do not mention in the report might be expected as questions from the members.

  a For some reason the income and expenditure account is for only 11 months, the year-end date having been brought forward by one month. This means that comparison with the previous full year's figures is difficult.
  b Profit on the hall bingo is substantially lower than last year.
  c Profit on the armchair bingo is substantially higher than last year.
  d Pool tables have produced much less income this year.
  e Team travelling expenses were a lot lower but players' expenses were considerably higher.

f Equipment repairs and renewals have cost much less this year.

g Not holding an annual dinner helped to save nearly £1000.

h Last year's large surplus of £5568 could not be maintained and this year income failed to cover expenditure leading to a deficit of £383.

i Without comparative figures for the balance sheet it is difficult to make general statements about the state of the club, but with an accumulated fund of £124771, and a loan outstanding of only £11401, it looks very healthy.

End-of-year
accounts for a
club.

Southern Cross

Athletic Club

Balance sheet 30 April, 1985

Assets		£	£
Hall	Valuation		50 000
Field	Valuation	27 155	
	New floodlights, railing	2 635	29 790
Buildings	Valuation		27 025
Fixtures and fittings	As at 1 June 1984	16 960	
	New fans	611	
		17 571	
	10% depreciation	1 611	15 960
Lawn mower	As at 1 June 1984	77	
	10% depreciation	7	70
P.A. System	As at 1 June 1984	69	
	20% depreciation	13	56
Committee room	Valuation		200
Drive tractor	As at 1 June 1984	562	
	25% depreciation	129	433
Microwave	As at 1 June 1984	205	
	20% depreciation	38	167
Premium bonds			100
Stock in hand	Bingo books	1 000	
	Buffet	1 475	
	Fruit cards	240	
	Footballs, etc.	750	
	Social club	2 050	5 515
Cash at bank			6 856
Total assets			£ 136 172
Represented by			
Accumulated fund			124 771
Bank loan			11 401
			£ 136 172

Value of all assets owned by club on date of balance sheet

Amount owing to bank

Value of club assets due to club members

Southern Cross

Athletic Club

Income and expenditure account

for the period 1 June 1984 to 30 April 1985

Income				Expenditure			
		12 months to 31.5.84					12 months to 31.5.84
		£	£			£	£
Hall bingo profit		2 621	3 801	Upkeep and maintenance – field		4 181	3 955
Armchair bingo profit		927	2 574	Upkeep hall		988	577
Fruit machine card profit		1 149	1 539	Advertising, printing, stationery and telephone		1 280	1 749
Buffet profit, hall and field		1 120	1 418	Team travelling expenses		1 023	2 079
Membership fees		1 583	1 785	Equipment repairs and renewals		3 496	4 724
League gate receipts		365	662	Medical expenses		339	258
Social club trading profit		15 149	15 833	Honorariums		500	500
				Laundry and cleaning of kits		410	252
Donations		500	350	Minibus and tractor expenses		319	678
Collections		–	208	Annual dinner expenses		–	922
Sale of mowers		–	150	Loan interest		1 834	1 985
Pool tables		548	1 119	Players expenses		3 666	1 015
Sponsorship		367	–	Bank interest and charges		296	527
Film horse racing		237	–	Club licence		15	15
Sale of bus		50	–	Insurance		964	102
				Hire of training ground		365	117
Fund-raising events				County fees		177	87
				Legal fees		–	115
Christmas raffle	634			Bar equipment and cleaning expenses		1 811	1 573
Easter raffle	119	753	1 054	Upkeep of social club		1 429	1 532
				Trophies and medals		341	165
		25 369	30 493	Entertaining visiting teams		323	148
				French visit – August 1984		299	–
Net expenditure over income for the period		383	–	Audit and accountancy		275	–
				Club fees and expenses			
				Hockey	175		194
				Whist drives	25		10
		£ 25 752	£ 30 493	Athletics	318		1 096
				Pool	14		29
				Darts	483		160
				Netball	406	1 421	361
				Net income over expenditure for the year		25 752	24 925
						–	5 568
						£ 25 752	£ 30 493

Activity 7	A friend of yours is thinking of investing in one of two manufacturing companies. Summarized accounts for the two companies are shown below. Write your advice to your friend, outlining with sound financial reasoning which company you would choose and the advantages and disadvantages of each one.

Balance sheet at 30 September 1986

	Factors and Co.		Makit and Co.	
	£'000	£'000	£'000	£'000
Freehold property at revaluation 1986		9 800		—
Plant, machinery and equipment at cost	8 400		11 200	
depreciation	7 700	700	2 800	8 400
Goodwill		—		4 200
Stocks: finished goods		1 400		700
work in progress		2 800		1 400
Debtors		6 300		2 800
Bank deposit		—		4 200
		21 000		21 700
less Creditors	6 300		4 900	
Overdraft	2 100	8 400	—	4 900
		12 600		16 800
Capital		9 100		10 500
Loans		3 500		6 300
		12 600		16 800
Additional information				
Sales		14 000		14 000
Net profit		2 800		3 500

Activity 8

A local business is operated by a trader as a 'one-man' business or sole trader.

Compare the performance for the past two years by calculating ratios. Explain what has happened to the business over the two-year period (see the note on the next page).

		Year 1 £		Year 2 £
Opening Stock		—		10 000
Purchases		80 000		119 500
Closing stock		10 000		15 500
Sales		100 000		150 000
Gross profit		30 000		36 000
Operating expenses		18 000		20 000
Net profit		£12 000		£16 000
Balance sheet information				
Fixed assets		11 000		10 000
Working capital				
Stock	10 000		15 500	
Debtors	8 000		13 500	
Cash	2 000	20 000	—	29 000
Creditors		7 000		11 000
Bank		—		2 000
		13 000		16 000
Capital		24 000		24 000
Add Net profit		12 000		16 000
		36 000		40 000
Less Drawings		12 000		14 000
		£24 000		£26 000

Before you begin make sure you understand the following terms:

gross profit
net profit
fixed assets
working capital
creditors
drawings.

It may be helpful to make notes on the meanings of these terms first, then look at the ratios of performance that could be calculated.

Activity 9 | Mr Johnson has had his accounts prepared. They are shown below.

Profit and loss account for the year to 31 December 1987

	£	£
Opening stock		20 000
Purchases		65 000
		85 000
Closing stock		25 000
Cost of sales		60 000
Sales		110 000
Gross profit		50 000
Wages	19 000	
Depreciation	8 000	
Expenses	6 200	
Loan interest	3 000	
Bad debts and increase in provision	900	
Advertising and promotional campaign	1 500	38 600
Net profit		£11 400

Balance sheet as at 31 December 1987

	£	£
Freehold land and buildings		40 000
Machinery and equipment at cost	75 000	
Less Depreciation to date	51 000	24 000
		64 000
Stock	23 000	
Debtors (£30 000 *less* provision 12 000)	18 000	
Bank	3 000	
	44 000	
Creditors and accruals	14 000	30 000
		£94 000
Johnson's capital at beginning of year	78 000	
Add Net profit	11 400	
	89 400	
Less Drawings	14 400	
	75 000	
Loan at 10% interest	19 000	£94 000

Working individually prepare notes for discussion on the following points:

a Are the accounts for the business or for Mr Johnson as an individual?

b Do the accounts reveal much information about the financial situation of Mr Johnson as an individual?

c How will the 'going concern' concept have affected the preparation of the accounts?

d What other concepts and conventions will have been used in preparing the accounts? List them and say how they would have been used.

e Is the worth of the business revealed by the balance sheet? Can you rely on this?

f Do you think the business is healthy as revealed by the

information in the profit and loss account and balance
sheet?

g How do you think the figure for depreciation might
have been arrived at?

h How do you think the materiality concept has affected
the valuation of assets?

Conclusion

At the beginning of this block, we mentioned three types of
organization: The High Street Motor Company, the
Meadowside Cricket Club and Football Club, and the Uphill
Technical College. Because only the first of these three can be
seen as a 'trading organization', most of the detail about
records and accounts has been concerned with businesses or
activities of this kind.

The accounting requirements of the sports club and the
technical college are quite different. The organizations serve
different purposes and raise income in a totally different way.
The sports club and other 'non-trading' organizations are the
subject of Block 10, but you may care to look at the accounts
of a sports club illustrated in Block 10 now. The context is
different to a trading organization but the function and
purpose is exactly the same.

The technical college will perhaps be a suitable type of
activity to study yourself. If you are studying on a full-time
or part-time course your fees will have been part of the
college's revenue. Whether you paid the fees yourself, or if
the local authority paid them, or indeed any other
organization, is to some extent irrelevant. The fees go
towards making up the college's income. The college
however will be part of the education provision provided by
your local authority and this provides you with a good
opportunity to enquire at the council, through local
councillors, about the allocation of funds to education in
general and the college in particular.

Block 5
Costing

Introduction

Financial and accounting information takes many different forms. Some information is provided solely for use by people and organizations that are outside the business providing the financial information, for example shareholders. The Inland Revenue requires accounting statements from the owners of businesses so that it can assess tax to be paid. Similarly the Inland Revenue requires information to be provided by private individuals so that their tax can be assessed and paid. Potential shareholders need to look at the annual reports and published accounts of businesses and these documents are freely available.

The financial information needed by business managers, to enable them to have more knowledge about events, is different from the information provided to the Inland Revenue and to shareholders. Managers need to know in much more detail the sources of profits in their firm. Which products are making profits? Which departments are operating effectively? In addition decisions have to be made and each decision will have financial implications. An accounting function within an organization needs to provide detailed information that can help in these areas.

Costing

Cost accounting or **costing** is part of the accounting function. It is concerned with providing information on operating costs for divisions, departments, activities and products.

Many textbooks on costing tend to deal with its benefits in manufacturing businesses. It is true that the development of industry and the growth of manufacturing companies in the early part of this century encouraged the development of costing: managers in these businesses needed to have more detailed information available. But nowadays there is a need for financial information in all types of business. We all have to be aware of costs, therefore cost information will need to be produced for individuals, for clubs, societies, and a variety of publicly and privately owned organizations. Farming (a primary industry), hospitals, hotels, colleges, schools and shops (service industries) all need to be efficient in using financial resources. Costing information helps such organizations. Costs need to be known for these industries and the following list will give some indication of the types of cost information needed:

A farm

cost of each crop per acre
transport costs
marketing costs
animal feed costs

A manufacturing business

cost of operating each machine
cost of operating each department
administration costs
distribution costs
research and development costs

| *Activity 1* | Give your suggestions on the sort of cost information that would be needed for colleges, schools, hospitals, shops and sports recreation centres. You may find it very useful to visit these types of organizations in your area to find out more about how they operate. |

Activity 1 deals with just a few of the many different organizations that require cost information. There are certain general principles that will be common to all these organizations and we will look at these first before moving on to other activities.

Direct and indirect costs

Direct costs are those incurred for what might be regarded as the prime purpose of the business. For example, direct material, in a manufacturing business, is the material used in making each product. Direct wages are the wages paid to the employees who specifically produce the items manufactured. It follows then that indirect costs are all the other costs incurred in the business that cannot be directly traced into product costs. Indirect costs are called **overheads** and can be seen as the costs of operating the business as a whole, rather than specific costs of any one direct operation.

In a business that makes desks and chairs from timber, costs might be as follows:

Direct costs

Direct material: the timber plus glue, screws, nails, paint and varnish.
Direct wages: the wages paid to employees assembling the desks and chairs.

Indirect costs

In this business indirect costs will include rent, rates, telephones, insurances, heating, lighting, salaries paid to supervisors, foremen, designers, accountants, etc.

In finding out the overall cost of each desk and each chair, it should be possible to find out the direct cost very accurately. The problem will be that, to some extent, each item made has benefited from the provision of services that the overhead costs provide.

The costing problem is in being able to cost out these overheads accurately to each item produced. Because these costs are indirect they cannot be charged directly, so they are 'spread' into the costs of each unit produced, by using the following sorts of techniques.

Allocation and apportionment

These are terms used when spreading total overhead costs to each department of a business. If, as in our example business making desks and chairs, products are worked on in three departments, then the overhead costs of operating these three departments needs to be spread into the costs of the desks and chairs as they pass through the departments during manufacture. But overhead costs are really incurred, in many cases, for the business as a whole, rather than for any one department.

Overhead costs have to be apportioned, or spread, to departments and this will require finding a fair method of spreading the costs. For instance the total cost of rent and rates could be spread to each department on the basis of the size or floor area of that department. The costs of salaries for supervisors could be spread on the basis of the number of employees in each department.

The term **allocation** is used when an overhead cost can clearly be charged directly to a department.

The term **apportionment** is used when a reasonable, but in the end arbitrary, estimate is made in charging costs to a department.

<table>
<tr><td>*Activity 2*</td><td>Suggest possible methods for spreading or apportioning the costs of the following to each department in the furniture-making business described above:

machine maintenance costs,
telephone costs,
canteen costs,
insurance costs,
administration costs.

You will perhaps discover that there is no right or wrong way of doing this and to some extent you have a degree of choice. What needs to be remembered is that this degree of choice will affect the costs of each department – and therefore the cost of each product manufactured in each department.</td></tr>
</table>

The next task is to decide how much of the total overhead of each department should be added to the cost of each product that is manufactured in that department. Again a degree of choice exists. If you own a car and you take it to a garage for repairs, you will have to pay for the materials used and in addition there will be a labour charge. This 'labour' charge will not just be for the wage costs of the mechanics but will also include a cost for the use of garage facilities. In other words you are being charged for overhead costs. The cost that your repair covers is the direct cost of materials and labour plus a share of the garage's overheads. You are paying on a time basis: the longer the repair takes, the more of the facilities of the garage are being used by you, and the more you pay.

If we now take this costing idea back to the business making desks and chairs, it seems equally fair that the longer each desk or chair takes to be produced in each department, the more it should be costed with the overhead of that department.

| Activity 3 | In this business making furniture, suggest how each item would be costed for overheads if there are three departments, namely the Sawing department, Assembly department and Finishing department. The total overheads of the business for the coming year are expected to be as follows: |

	£
Rent	1 200
Rates	800
Salaries	12 000
Insurances	650
Telephone	1 350
Depreciation	8 000
Heat and light	2 500
Maintenance	3 500
	30 000

The assembly department takes up 50% of the total floor space with the other two departments taking up 25% each. There are 40 employees in the Sawing department, 25 in the Assembly department and 15 in the Finishing department.

Capital equipment costing £25 000 is in the Sawing department, and equipment costing £15 000 is in the Assembly department. During the year there should be 7 000 hours worked in the Sawing department, 4 000 in the Assembly department and 2 500 in the Finishing department.

This activity will show that it is possible to charge overhead costs to products but
a it is not an easy task and,
b the cost of each product is being influenced by the decisions that have to be made regarding apportioning overheads.

Having completed this activity you have hopefully produced something like this:

	Total £	Assembly £	Sawing £	Finishing £
Rent	1 200	600	300	300
Rates	800	400	200	200
Salaries	12 000	3 750	6 000	2 250
Premises insurance	650	325	162	163
Telephone	1 350	422	675	253
Depreciation	8 000	3 000	5 000	—
Heat and light	2 500	1 250	625	625
Maintenance	3 500	2 187	1 313	—
Total overhead costs	30 000	11 934	14 275	3 791

It is quite difficult to decide on the best and most suitable way to spread some of the overhead costs. This is a problem faced by all businesses in that there cannot be a 'right' or 'wrong' method. The method of spreading costs must in the end be based on opinion, but hopefully an opinion based on a careful consideration of the fairest method. In this case, the **overhead absorption rate** is given as follows:

$$\text{Overhead absorption rate} = \frac{\text{Total overheads for department}}{\text{Hours to be spent on production}}$$

This produces the following results:

	Assembly £	Sawing £	Finishing £
Total overhead costs	11 934	14 275	3 791
Hours to be spent on production	4 000	7 000	2 500
Overhead rates	2.98	2.04	1.52

If we now come to find out the cost of Desk Type 24 and we know the time taken in production is: Assembly department 2 hours, Sawing department 1/2 hour, and Finishing department 1 hour, the overhead cost of this desk will be as shown at the top of the next page.

		£
Assembly Department	2 hrs × £2.98	5.96
Sawing Department	½ hr × £2.04	1.02
Finishing Department	1 hr × £1.52	1.52
		8.50

To this the *direct* costs of material and wages will need to be added, to give the total costs.

To obtain these direct costs the business will need to keep careful records of the material used on each desk and chair, and also the employees will need to record their labour time on each activity.

Businesses that are not engaged in manufacturing have similar problems. If a sports centre wants to know how much profit is being made by the different sections it operates, it will first of all need to know the revenue earned by each section and then the costs of each section. The problem will be that some costs will be direct and specific to the section, others will not. These latter costs will be overhead costs for the sports centre as a whole and will have to be apportioned to each section. The profit of each section will then reflect the decision about how these overhead costs should be spread.

Some of the activities in Block 6 involve decision making based on a knowledge of costing. The costs that we have looked at in this block have been classified as either **direct** or **indirect**, but of course, they are exactly the same costs that could be classified as **fixed** or **variable**. Cost accounting is concerned with finding out costs for particular activities in any business, but in addition it is concerned with providing cost information for decision making. Block 6 deals with this decision-making side (including fixed and variable costs) but, in the same way as some of the activities in this block, it relies on costs being classified and recorded accurately.

Activity 4	Discuss with other students how you think the furniture business described earlier in this block might be able to record accurately the *direct costs* of each of its products.

If you have access to any local firms, try to collect documents that might help you in this activity. Documents such as **material requisitions** usually detail the type and quantity of material to be used on each product, and these are of course important for costing purposes.

Activity 5   List the overhead costs you think you would find in the following businesses:
a theatre,   a college or school,
a skiing centre,   a garage,
a garden centre,   a manufacturer of office furniture.

Activity 6   Taking the businesses listed in Activity 5, list the sort of costs that would be classed as direct.

Activity 7   One of your friends has decided to develop his part-time work into a full-time business of house painting and decorating.
a Discuss with other students what you think should be considered before starting this venture.
b Assuming your friend does start the business, he will need to make sure that he is paid by customers for the work that he does. Design a system that will enable him to cost each job accurately and charge each customer for the work done.
c Which costs are likely to be classed as direct in this business and which ones classed as indirect? Do you think that such a classification is important in a business such as this?

Conclusion

The subject of costing is vast and complicated. We have attempted to introduce some of the basic terms and ideas. It should at least be clear that an organization will wish to keep records in sufficient detail to calculate the cost of the job, product or service. Without this information managers have no idea whether the organization is profitable, or working within its budget, until it is too late. In later blocks we shall expand on some of the costing techniques which might be used, and it may repay you to read this block again towards the end of the course.

Block 6
Decision Making and
Cost Behaviour

Introduction: decision making and cost behaviour

Individuals and business organizations need to make many decisions. Information is needed to provide the decision maker with facts that will help him to make the right decision. Financial information will help particularly in making the following sorts of decision:

a **Make or buy** For example, should a manufacturing business make all the components it needs, or should it attempt to buy some of them from outside suppliers?

b **Pricing decisions** For example, what price should be charged for the goods and services offered?

c **Expansion or reduction decision** For example, should the business expand so as to be able to produce and sell more? Should it contract because of shortage of work?

d **Finance** How should new equipment be financed? Through loans, overdrafts, by leasing or by hire purchase?

e **Credit control** How should credit control be achieved?

These and other decisions require the decision maker to gather together facts and predictions logically and sensibly so as to be able to consider all possible alternatives. Financial data needs to be correct, available and *understood*.

Cost behaviour

Not all of the possible decisions listed above require information only about costs, but cost information is often very necessary to help the decision-making process. The term **cost behaviour** relates to the way different costs will be affected by changes in the quantity produced or sold. Costs can be seen as either **fixed, variable** or **semi-variable**.

Costs that are fixed will remain static irrespective of the volume of business undertaken by the firm.

Costs that are variable will increase as production increases and, of course, decrease as output falls.

Costs such as rent, rates, insurances and salaries of managers will be classed as fixed costs. Variable costs will be the costs that increase as output increases, and which are lower at lower levels of production or volume, e.g. component costs.

If you consider the costs of a transport firm, some costs, such as the petrol and diesel costs, will be classed as variable, because the more miles the transport fleet does, the higher will be the cost. In a manufacturing business variable costs will include the material used in producing the output. Fixed costs will include rates, telephone charges, insurances, etc.

Some costs may include both a fixed element and a variable element. Electricity, for example, is fixed in that lighting and heating are the same at most levels of output. As output rises however, the variable element of the electricity bill, that used for machine power, will also rise. This type of cost is known as semi-variable.

One way of considering and understanding whether costs are fixed or variable is to draw simple charts showing 'cost behaviour' and the output, or volume, of business.

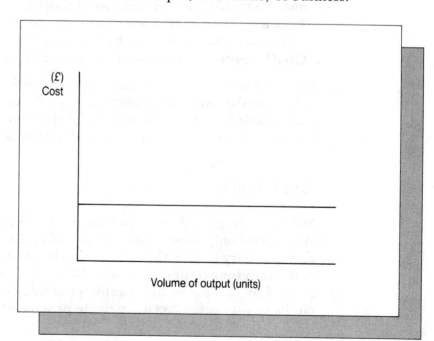

Fixed costs (e.g. rent, rates, staff salaries, insurance)

(£)
Cost

Volume of output (units)

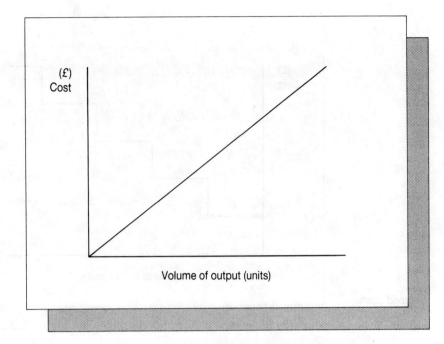

Variable costs (e.g. material used, electricity for machine power, some wages costs)

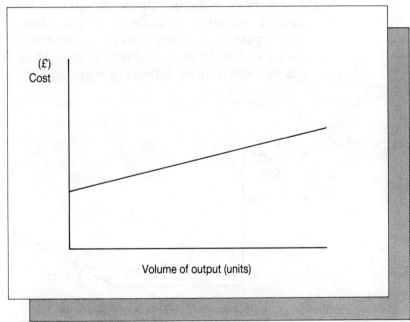

Semi-variable costs (e.g. the overall power bill)

Other costs are more difficult to classify. They may stay the same over a range of output and then rise suddenly in a single step, for instance supervision salaries if the number of supervisors has to increase to some extent as volume increases. These are sometimes referred to as **stepped costs**.

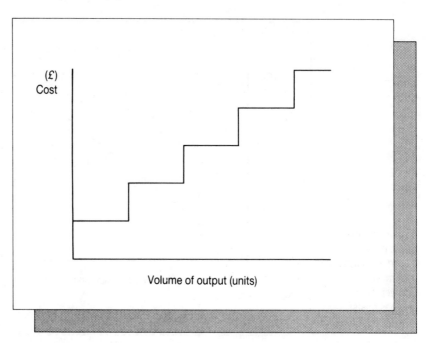

Stepped costs.

A variety of 'patterns' can be shown to suit different costs in different situations in different organizations. Think about the wages paid to salesmen who get a commission paid on sales after a certain level, in addition to their basic salary. This cost can be shown in the following way:

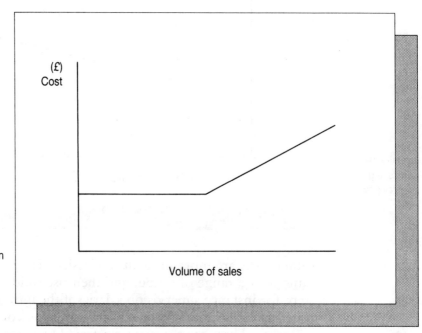

A fixed cost pattern changing to a variable cost pattern.

Note that the variable cost in the chart at the bottom of page 106 is now related to sales and not to output.

If you consider any situation, business or personal, it should generally be possible to classify costs into categories of fixed, variable or semi-variable. Remember, an exact categorization is not always possible and you may need to know a lot more about the specific business. A cost may be fixed in one business and variable in another. For instance wages may be paid as a fixed amount per month and paid as a salary in one firm, but in another firm wages may be paid according to output achieved.

Activity 1	This activity is designed to involve you in thinking about the sort of costs that might be incurred in different types of business.

Costs need to be understood by owners or managers in all types of business so that they can assess the effect on costs if certain decisions are made.

Draw charts like the one below with the *Volume of output* (or Activity) and *Costs* as the two axes.

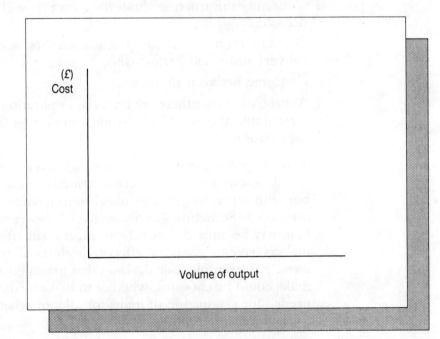

First list the costs you would expect to be incurred in the following businesses:

a an engineering firm,
b a local theatre,
c a local sports centre,
d a garden centre,
e a firm that designs, builds and rents out boats.

Now using charts like the one on page 107, plot the costs on to the charts to show whether you think they are fixed, variable or semi-variable.

Activity 2 List the costs you would incur if you owned and ran a car. Plot these costs on to charts, similar to those shown in this block, showing clearly the costs you think will be fixed and those that are either variable or semi-variable.

Show the 'activity' or 'volume' as miles.

Information about cost behaviour is important as one stage in collecting information that will help in decision making. Decision making in any business situation involves the following stages:

1 Collecting information about the facts that will influence a decision.
2 Deciding on technical and practical matters, such as quality, delivery times and performance.
3 Choosing between alternatives.
4 Appreciating that there are financial implications, and that these implications may be the most important features of the decision.

This last point about finance opens up a very wide area. A few decisions are made by considering financial aspects only, but with other decisions financial considerations will be less important. Sometimes decisions have long-term implications that may be quite different from short-term effects. Decision makers have to assess the effect in both the short and long term. For example, one decision that managers may have to make could be choosing whether to make a component needed for production of items for sale, or whether to buy it from an outside supplier.

Activity 3

A firm making stereo systems needs a particular speaker. This could be made in the firm, as they have the manpower, skill, materials and technology, but it could also be purchased from outside.

This activity involves you in making the decision whether to make or buy. There are of course many technical details that would have to be considered, as well as financial data. The financial data is given below. Read it through first, discuss it with others, and then try to make a decision as to whether to make or buy.

Costs of making a speaker

	£
Direct material	6.90
Direct labour	4.50 (2 hours at £2.25 per hour)
Variable overhead	2.20
Fixed overhead	4.00
Total cost	17.60

The figure of £4 for fixed overhead is arrived at as the 'share' of overhead to be carried by this speaker. The fixed overhead costs in the business are as follows:

	£
Rent	1 200
Rates	2 300
Depreciation of equipment	3 400
Telephone	1 450
Insurances	850
Staff salaries	9 500
Heat and light	1 300
Total	20 000

In the year the firm expects to work for ten thousand hours. These are the hours to be spent on producing all products in the firm, including the speakers.

Having estimated its fixed overhead costs of £20 000 the firm will try to spread these costs into the costs of each product that is produced. The firm is expecting to work ten thousand hours on production so the fixed overhead cost will be £2 per hour. The speaker takes two hours to be manufactured so £4 must be added to its direct costs for fixed overhead (see Block 5 for a discussion on this).

If the firm could buy from an outside supplier a similar
speaker for £14.80, should it do so? Consider the cost
implications and any other effects. In this activity you are
provided with financial data alone, but there will be
other considerations, for example technical aspects and
effects on the labour force.

Contribution

We have seen that some costs in a business are fixed and these
will remain fixed irrespective of whether or not the volume of
output or level of activity increases or decreases. Other costs
are variable. They are the sort of costs that will increase or
decrease with the output or volume of the business. Product
costs, such as direct materials, are variable, as will be the
petrol costs for coach operators.

It is possible to charge fixed costs into the cost of each
product, but this can be a misleading figure as the cost will
remain fixed *in total* in the business whether a particular
product is made or not.

Contribution = Sales revenue *less* Variable cost

Contribution then is the difference between the specific sales
revenue of a particular product or activity and the variable
cost of that product or activity. Contributions go towards
paying off the fixed costs of the business. What is left is then
profit. If a firm makes three products we can illustrate
contribution as follows:

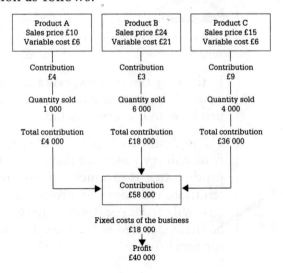

This can be described as using what is sometimes called the **marginal cost equation**:

Sales		**Fixed cost**
less	= **Contribution** =	***plus***
Variable costs		**Profit**

$$S - V = C = F + P$$

An accountant would present these figures in a form easily understood by management.

Budgeted cost statement for products A, B and C:

	A	B	C	Total
	£	£	£	£
Sales	10 000	144 000	60 000	214 000
Less Variable costs	6 000	126 000	24 000	156 000
Contribution	4 000	18 000	36 000	58 000
Less Fixed costs	—	—	—	18 000
Profit				40 000

The following activities are concerned with the concept of contribution and the way it can help decision making.

Activity 4

A firm has a profit requirement for the present year of £30 000 and its maximum capacity is to produce 30 000 units of its product. So far it has orders as follows:
a from Company A, 10 000 at £6 each;
b from Company B, 8 000 at £5.50 each;
c from Company C, 6 000 at £5 each.

The variable cost of making and selling each unit is £3 and the fixed cost for the business are £41 000 per year. What would be the lowest price at which the production that is not yet on order could be sold for if the company is to meet its profit requirement?

Activity 5

With other students, discuss how you think a knowledge of cost behaviour might help you in running a small hotel, with particular reference to the problem of fixing charges to customers and the controlling of all the costs of operating the hotel.

| *Activity 6* | The information given below is for two companies. Which of the two do you think will be the more profitable if, *a* sales demand is very low? *b* sales demand is very high? |

	Company X		**Company Y**	
	£	£	£	£
Sales		1 500 000		1 500 000
Costs				
Variable	500 000		900 000	
Fixed	600 000	1 100 000	200 000	1 100 000
Profit		400 000		400 000

Break-even analyses and break-even charts

Recognizing that costs 'behave' in a variety of fashions, as illustrated by your activities, you can see that it is possible to predict the total costs expected to be incurred in a business at different levels (volumes) of sales. If sales revenue can be predicted it is possible to show on a chart the profits or losses that are expected at different sales levels in the business. If you consider first of all the revenue from sales it should look like this on a chart:

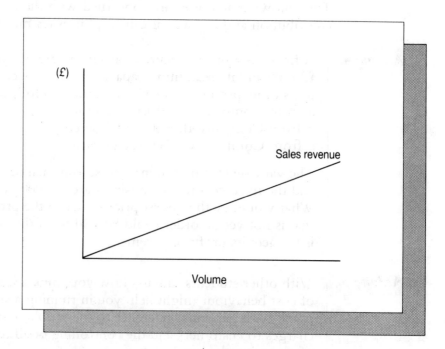

Sales revenue.

Costs, as we have seen, will be both fixed and variable and so total costs for a business will look like this.

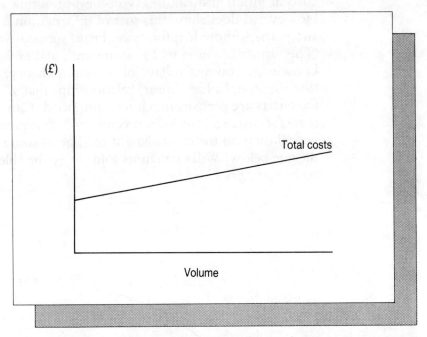

Total costs.

By putting both sales revenue and costs together on the same chart a **break-even chart** can be produced. This shows the point where the sales line and the total costs line cross.

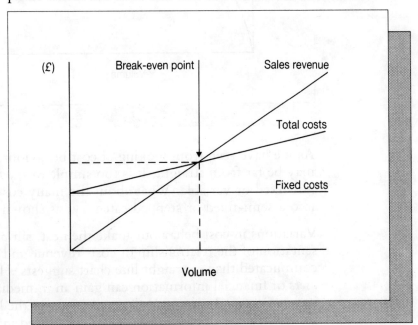

A break-even chart.

Such a chart does not give any extra information that could
not be obtained from simply listing sales revenue and total
costs at different quantities (volumes) of output and sales.
However it does show this sort of information in a different,
and perhaps more helpful, way. From some of your studies of
'The Organization in its Environment', and perhaps from any
knowledge you might have of economic theory, you can see
that the straight line (linear) relationships that are shown on
the charts are perhaps much too simplified. Can we be certain
that, for instance, the sales revenue will always increase in the
way shown on the chart? Might the line in some cases be like
the one below? Will extra units sold always be able to be sold
at the same price?

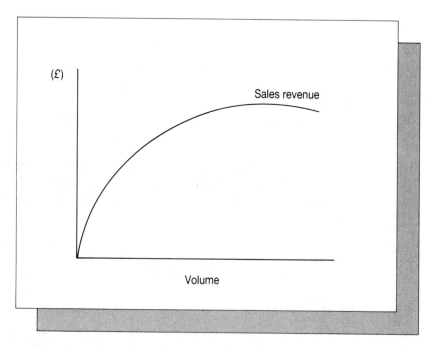

As we have seen from looking at cost behaviour, cost lines
may be far from straight. It is too simple to say that costs are
just fixed or variable. What about the many costs that come
into a semi-fixed or stepped category, as shown opposite?

Variations in cost behaviour make the neat, simple presentation of the relationship of cost, revenue and profit more
complicated than a straight line chart suggests. However the
users of financial information can gain an immediate
impression, and, provided they are aware of the limitations,
benefits can be obtained from charts produced in this way.

Stepped costs.

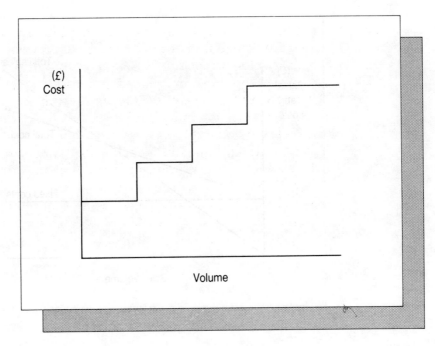

Semi-fixed costs.

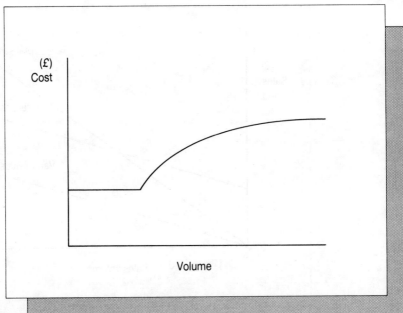

Activity 7 | The two charts on the next page are for the same business and show exactly the same situation, i.e. total costs and sales revenue for last year's results, but they are shown in different ways. Explain the benefits, and any problems you think exist, with charts presented in these ways.

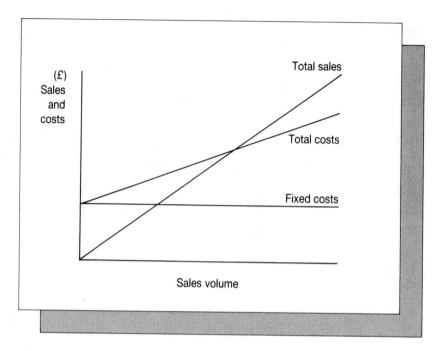

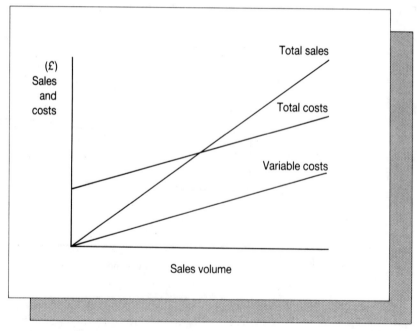

Activity 8

Draw a break-even chart for the Sparko Manufacturing Company. It produces only one product: the Sparko. The product costs are:
direct material per unit, £6,
direct labour per unit, £3.

The fixed costs for the business are £25 000 for the year, and the Sparko product sells for £14.
If the firm expects to produce and sell 8 000 units, what do you think its **margin of safety** is?

As you may have guessed from the name, the margin of safety is the amount of sales which the firm can lose while still breaking even. It may be expressed as a number of units or as a turnover figure.

The chart you may have produced for Activity 8 is no doubt very clear and has straight lines. Do you think in a more complicated business, perhaps one with many different activities, and producing many different products, it would be as easy to produce a chart that looked like yours?

The following activities are suggestions for work which will bring together some of the things discussed in this block, but they may make you look for yourself at other businesses and situations, and therefore widen your understanding.

Activity 9

Imagine you have been given the job of assisting the manager of a new ice rink that has just been built in your area. You need to ensure that the rink is profitable.

Prepare a report to the manager on all the items that you think should receive careful attention in trying to ensure profitability. Perhaps a listing of possible costs might help, with an explanation of the nature of the cost. Similarly the policies for gaining revenue or income should be carefully examined.

Activity 10

Your local supermarket has always charged customers for plastic carrier bags; the bags are covered with advertising slogans for the supermarket chain. A recent consumer programme on local radio has featured this policy as being unfair to customers.
a Discuss with other students alternative policies that the supermarket could try, and summarize your discussions in a suitable form so that the management of the supermarket could consider them.
b Visit local supermarkets and ascertain their policies on carrier bags and whether they charge for them. Assemble your findings in a logical manner and discuss them with other students.

Activity 11

The concept of *contribution* is very important as a means of assessing true profitability of separate activities in any business. Be certain that you understand what this term means before you attempt this activity.

A firm has a profit requirement for the present financial year of £80 000. It has capacity to produce 3 000 of its product. So far it has orders as follows:

1 300 to company A, at £95 each,

700 to company B, at £100 each.

A special order at £25 000 for 480 units of especially high quality as a loss leader for a new customer. This would involve the modification of a machine at a once only cost of £3 000.

The variable cost of making and selling each unit is £43 and fixed costs are £32 000 for the year.

a Calculate the lowest price that the uncommitted production could be sold for. What difference does the acceptance or rejection of the special order make?

b Having calculated a proposed selling price, discuss with other students the factors other than cost that would usually influence the selling price of a product.

Activity 12

The chart shown below is given to you when you attend an interview for a position in the finance department of a local manufacturing company.

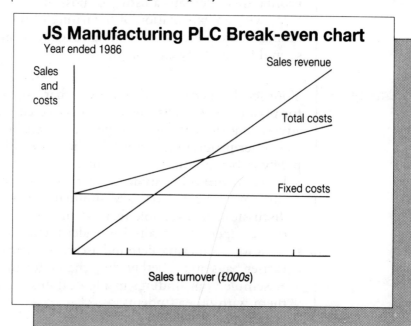

JS Manufacturing PLC: break-even chart for year end 1986.

The Chief Accountant and Training Officer have decided in interviewing to use the approach of a test for candidates that will assess their ability to answer technical questions. In this case the Chief Accountant says to you: 'As you can see from the chart, last year we broke even when sales were £250 000. This year we are budgeted to achieve sales of £390 000, so we should have a very profitable year. Do you agree?'

Before you came to the interview you did some research and found out that the company operates in three main areas. It produces drilling rods for the mining industry and it also hires out equipment for small exploration projects. Any spare capacity is taken up by carrying out sub–contract manufacturing for larger firms.

You are told also that last year the sales were £250 000 and the company broke even with these sales made up of:

	Sales	% Contribution to sales
	£	£
Drill rod manufacture	150 000	40%
Hire	60 000	30%
Sub-contract	40 000	20%
	250 000	
Fixed costs were	£86 000	

For the coming year the 'margin' for contribution is expected to remain the same for each of the three groups and the £390 000 sales is expected to be made up as below:

	£
Drill rod manufacture	160 000
Hire	120 000
Sub-contract	110 000
	390 000

Prepare the answer that you think you ought to give.

Activity 11	Make notes listing the differences between **marginal costing**, and **full** or **total absorption costing**, as described in Block 5.
	Your notes should include features regarding the nature and treatment of fixed costs in a business, and a list of the sort of costs that you might expect to be fixed in different businesses.
Activity 12	In producing this book the publishers incurred costs. What sort of costs do you think they were? Which might be classed as *fixed* and which might be *variable*?

Block 7
Stock Control

Introduction

Businesses need to hold stocks, so that they can have supplies readily available for use, either to sell directly to customers if they are a retailer, or to convert into finished products if they are a manufacturing business.

Stock control

The flow of money involved with stocks for a manufacturing business looks like the diagram below:

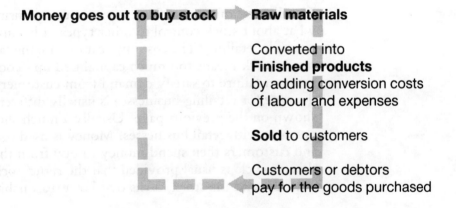

Money goes out to buy stock ➤ **Raw materials**

Converted into
Finished products
by adding conversion costs
of labour and expenses

Sold to customers

Customers or debtors
pay for the goods purchased

There is a cycle of funds moving in a business. Money goes out to buy raw materials and money eventually comes back in from customers who have bought the finished products.

This cycle is part of what accountants call the **working capital cycle**. All this means is that some capital in a business is in the form of plant, machinery and buildings: fixed assets as defined in Block 4. Other capital is more 'liquid' in that it changes its form more rapidly. In the illustration above, raw material stock becomes finished goods stock, which becomes payments due from debtors when sold, and becomes cash when customers pay.

However, there is a cost to holding stock. Businesses have to keep stock, but the costs of doing so can be high. Investing capital in stock means losing any interest that could have been earned by investing the funds elsewhere. There are costs of storage, risks of deterioration, obsolescence, administration and insurance costs.

In simple terms, if a business invests in more stock than it really needs, or invests in stock that is 'slow-moving', or worse still 'never-moving', then a lot of money can be tied up that could be used more usefully elsewhere.

What this implies, of course, is that careful controls on stock levels need to be developed. The right amounts of stock need to be available at the right times. But what will be the right amount? This is not really a question that can be answered without a detailed knowledge of a firm, its products, suppliers, rate of usage of material, etc., but it is a calculation that needs to be done on all businesses.

The illustration used is for a manufacturing business, but what about stock control in other types of business, for example retailing? The cost implications are the same: too much stock means too much capital tied up. Too little stock means a failure to satisfy demand from customers. However, the *cycle* for retailing businesses is usually different from that shown on the previous page. Usually a much shorter cycle operates with retail businesses. Money is used to obtain stock and customers then spend money to buy from the retailer. A shorter cycle is usual provided that the right stocks are available and the stock 'turns over' at a reasonable rate.

| *Activity 1* | Draw a flow chart similar to that on page 121 showing the movement of money both in and out of a firm in relation to stock. Draw one for both a retailer and for a manufacturer and discuss with other students the periods that might be involved between money going out and money coming back in. |

In order to ensure that money returns to the organization as quickly as possible, it is important to keep a careful check on payments due from customers. Delayed payment by customers will extend the cycle and adversely affect the cash flow. Checking on payments due is the work of credit controllers; there is an account of their work in Block 12.

Part of the problem with material and stock control is that some items of stock are used more frequently than others. These items therefore have to be replaced more frequently. In the case of a supermarket for example, there are large stocks of some popular items and small stocks of specialist items. A lot of money can be tied up keeping such a large quantity and range of stock. Slow-moving stocks can be a considerable problem as items on shelves represent an investment; when sold they represent cash. How much of an asset is stock, particularly if it has been held for a long time?

Stock control software packages are a popular computer item. They are generally fairly simple to operate and they are designed to give detailed and essential figures for all items of stock held by a business. The more detailed software packages are designed to show all material received, issues from stock, and a balance of stock at any point in time. They also generally indicate a **re-order level** or **minimum stock level**, that is the level of stock at which an order should be placed for replacement stock.

Activity 2	If you have stock control software packages available at your college or place of work, ask to see one operating. Look at the print-out and see what sort of information it gives. More importantly perhaps, you should discuss with other students the sort of information it should give.

It really does not matter whether or not computers are used to give this sort of information. What is important is the information, not the means of producing it. Documents (something like the one below) need to be available to give that information.

Stock Item   Name ....

Stock No. ....

Re-order Level ....   Re-order Quantity ....

Date	Receipts			Issues			Balance			
	Qty.	Unit Price	Total	Qty.	Unit Price	Total	Qty.	Unit Price	Total	

Document for a manual stock system.

A	B	C	D	E	F	G	H	I	J	K
STOCK SERIAL NUMBER	STOCK NAME	SUPPLIER NAME	SUPPLIER CODE	LOCATION CODE	PRICE	QUANTITY UNITS	QUANTITY IN STOCK	MINIMUM QUANTITY	REORDER QUANTITY	STOCK ITEM BULK
1	4 OHM RESISTOR	A. W. PETERS	EM01	ER506	.530	BOX OF 10	406	100	529	10
2	7.5 MICROFARAD CAPACITOR	A. W. PETERS	EM01	EC995	.480		334	50	1183	1
3	250 MICROHENRY INDUCTOR	A. W. PETERS	EM01	EI510	4.220		471	50	374	10
4	64 BIT MICROPROCESSOR	FERRANTI	EL01	IC573	2.710		799	500	1183	10
5	OSCILLOSCOPE	MACROELECTRONICS LTD	EL02	ET612	206.800		5	2	1	100000
6	24-CORE DATA CABLE	BICC	LM01	LC444	2.460	METER	901	200	167	200
7	16 GAGE ENAMELLED WIRE	BICC	LM01	LC595	.086	METER	797	600	1296	10
8	PHILLIPS SCREWDRIVER	LOCAL IRONMONGERS LTD	GM01	GT377	1.500		25	30	65	200
9	SCREWDRIVER	LOCAL IRONMONGERS LTD	GM01	GT696	1.250		44	40	75	200
10	3 TO 25.5 VARIABLE CAPACITANCE	MACROELECTRONICS	EL02	EC113	3.710		32	55	88	200
11	SOLDERING IRON	LOCAL IRONMONGERS	GM01	GT344	6.700		12	15	46	200
12	240V to 12V TRANSFORMER	MIDLAND ELECTRICAL CO	LM02	LT844	2.570		79	20	53	200
13	240V THREE-TAP TRANSFORMER	MIDLAND ELECTRICAL CO	LM02	LT203	9.900		89	8	33	200
14	THYRISTOR	MACROELECTRONICS LTD	EL02	ET674	3.060		63	10	167	10
15	THERMIONIC PENTODE	MACROELECTRONICS LTD	EL02	ET493	1.630		37	5	118	10
16	TRANSISTOR DIODE	MACROELECTRONICS LTD	EL02	ED710	2.800	BOX OF 5	72	100	1673	1

A spreadsheet for a computerized stock system.

In contrast, a print-out from a spreadsheet package in use for stock control is shown above. Spreadsheet packages are particularly suitable for this kind of application. Suppliers are listed, as are other details, such as the Supplier's Code, and the Stores Location Code indicating where the items can be found in the stores.

The benefit of keeping this information on a computer spreadsheet is that once the basic information has been input, it can be easily updated to reflect the inward and outward movement of stock.

Activity 3

Look back now at the activity ratios described in Block 4, in particular the rate of stock turnover. It is important to understand how to calculate this ratio and to be able to analyse different rates of stock turnover in different businesses.

It may help to illustrate stock usage by showing the different patterns on a simple chart.

The chart opposite (top) shows an item of stock that is used a lot and therefore needs to be replenished frequently. This item of material has an *even* pattern. It is consumed, or used, evenly and it can be replaced to a similar

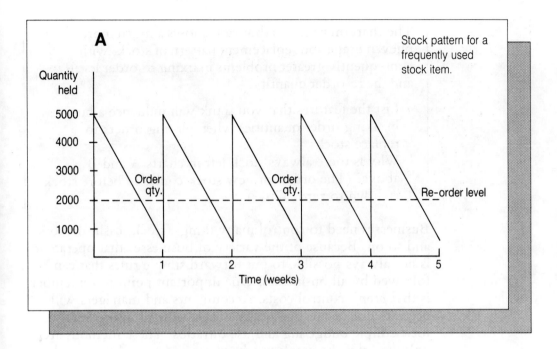

A

Stock pattern for a frequently used stock item.

Quantity held

5000
4000
3000
Order qty.
Order qty.
2000 — — — — — — — — — — — — — — — — — — — Re-order level
1000

Time (weeks)

pattern. This should make stock control easier. Of course most firms will need to keep a wide range of stock items; some will be used rapidly, others will not. In such a situation, stock control is more complex.

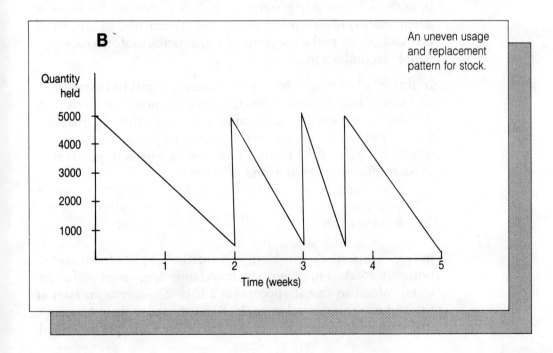

B

An uneven usage and replacement pattern for stock.

Quantity held

5000
4000
3000
2000
1000

Time (weeks)

> The chart on page 125 (bottom) shows a much more uneven usage and replacement pattern of stock, with consequently greater problems in fixing re-order levels and the re-order quantity.
>
> a List the features that you think will influence a business in fixing order quantities when placing orders to replace stocks.
> b Why is there always stock left in charts A and B above? (The order for new stock comes in before stock is down to zero. Why?)

Businesses need to control many things: stock, cash, debtors and so on. Because of the variety of businesses that operate it is not always possible to put forward simple rules that can be followed by all businesses. One important point to remember is that *people* control costs. Accountants and managers will need to look for techniques to enable control to be exercised, for example budgeting and use of ratios. These methods are only useful if the *people* in a business understand them and have enough information to make effective control possible. It is essential for us all to remember that as people we are all different; we are restricted by different things and can understand some things more easily than others. In the area of financial control many good managers have blind spots about finance and accounting statements. It is important for finance departments, in designing forms and statements, to recognize this and try to make accounting and financial information simple to understand.

In this block we have been considering control of materials and stock, but the same principle that it is *people* in a business that exercise control applies equally to other areas of finance. Control procedures have vital financial implications so an important part of the financial manager's role is to get over these implications clearly and effectively.

Stock valuation

In any business, the problem of valuation applies to all assets, not only stock. However, stock certainly is an asset and needs to be valued so that it appears on a balance sheet as an asset at the end of the financial year. In Block 1, accounting concepts and conventions are discussed. One of the concepts described is **prudence**, and it is this concept which applies particularly in valuing all assets. Stock is therefore valued according to the general rule of the lower of **cost** or **net realizable value**.

Stock is valued at the lower of cost *or* net realizable value

This means stock will be valued *not* at what it could be sold for, but at cost – unless of course the available market price (the net realizable value) had dropped below the cost price. Normal business practice should of course mean that stock is valued at cost. But what is the cost? Consider the following.

A company buys and issues stock as follows:

3 January	300 units at £1 each
19 January	200 units at £1.10 each
25 January	200 units at £1.15 each
26 January	issued from stock 150 units

If we produce this information on a stock record card, or as an account, it will appear like this:

Date	Receipts			Issues			Balance		
	Qty.	Price	Total £	Qty.	Price	Total £	Qty.	Price	Total
3 Jan	300	£1	300				300	£1	300
19 Jan	200	£1.10	220				300	£1	300
							200	£1.10	220
							500		520
25 Jan	200	£1.15	£230				300	£1	300
							200	£1.10	220
							200	£1.15	230
							700		750
26 Jan				200	£1	200	100	£1	100
							200	£1.10	220
							200	£1.15	230
							500		550

A stock account.

The issues of 200 units have been valued at £1 each, the first cost incurred, leaving the units in stock valued at the other prices paid. This is a **first in–first out**, or **FIFO**, basis. This method assumes a chronological order for issuing. Is this fair and is it right? At times of inflation the effect of using this method is for issues to be made at old and 'out of date' prices not reflecting 'current' prices that have to be paid. But of course stock that is left will be valued at costs that include the more recent purchases.

An alternative would be to use the opposite method of **last in–first out**, or **LIFO**, whereby the most recent stock prices are issued first.

| *Activity 4* | Complete the Stock Account on page 127 using the LIFO method and compare the value of the 500 units left in stock. |

A further possibility would be to average the prices so that issues from stock are at an **average cost** for all the purchases and similarly the stock that remains is valued at an average cost. The average price is worked out each time material is received. The account would then be like this:

Date	Receipts			Issues			Balance		
	Qty.	Price	Total	Qty.	Price	Total	Qty.	Price	Total
			£			£			
31 Jan	300	1	300				300	1	300
19 Jan	200	1.10	220				300	1.04	520
25 Jan	200	1.15	230				700	1.07	750
26 Jan				200	1.07	214	500	1.07	536

Each of the three methods, FIFO, LIFO, and average cost, values stock at cost.

FIFO, LIFO and average cost

The stock account on page 127 has used a FIFO approach by issuing stock values in chronological order. LIFO would take the opposite approach by issuing the most recently required prices first, ensuring that issues are always at an up-to-date price, more readily reflecting current costs. At times of inflation this means that profits will also reflect current purchasing costs. Consider the following FIFO example:

Purchases

8 January	100 at £5 each
14 January	200 at £5.50 each
20 January	100 at £6 each

Sales

End of January   100 units at £8 each

		£
Sales	100 at £8	800
Cost of sales	100 at £5	500
	Profit	**300**
Stock	200 × £5.50	1 100
	100 × £6	600
		1 700

If a LIFO method had been used the profit for the company would have been as follows:

		£
Sales	100 at £8	800
Cost of sales	100 at £6	600
	Profit	**200**
Stock	200 × £5.50	1 100
	100 × £5.00	500
		1 600

We have two different profit figures and two different valuations of stock, both at cost but both at a different cost. We also have two different profit figures. It is the same company selling the same goods to the same customers and with the same stock remaining, but there are different results, dependent upon which valuation method is used.

| Activity 5 | a Calculate the profit and the stock valuation for the case shown on page 129 using the average cost method of valuation. |
| | b Which of the stock valuation methods do you think is the fairest and why? List the features you think are important. |

Activity 6	Collect the published accounts or annual reports of as many companies as you can. Find out what the *notes on the accounts* say about the valuation of stock.
	Compare your findings with other students and explain what the notes really tell you about the valuation method.
	If you have information from firms in different industries or engaged in a wide range of different activities, do you think it likely they all use the same valuation methods?

Block 8
Organizing a Business Conference

Introduction

The organization of a single event or function can teach us many lessons regarding the principles of finance. For the purposes of this block we are going to imagine that you have been asked by your employer to organize a two-day business conference in a town near to your home.

The conference

The conference will involve supervisors and managers from other organizations attending four sessions, two mornings and two afternoons on successive days in a hotel or conference centre. You expect to attract many clients locally and they will attend the four sessions and lunch on each day. Delegates attending the meetings from a distance will need accommodation and an evening meal during the conference.

In addition to the involvement of two members of your own staff to run the conference, you are going to hire two visiting lecturers, one from the local technical college and one from industry, to provide the technical expertise for the event.

Activity 1	Your organization will only run this event if there is a fair chance that it will make a profit. Without specifying the amounts, list in detail all items of *income* and all items of *expenditure* involved in the running of such an event, stating whether the expenses are fixed or variable.

As is often the case, you will have discovered in doing Activity 1 that whereas there are unlikely to be many sources of income for such an event (probably only the fees from the delegates, unless you considered some form of sponsorship), there are many different classes of expenditure.

This is a common situation in all areas of finance and is the main reason why it is so important to keep control over costs, especially since costing figures are often complicated. The costs which you listed for Activity 1, for example, should have included fees for the visiting lecturers, hire of rooms, meals, refreshments, stationery and many others.

| Activity 2 | Find out the approximate prices of the hotels, conference centres or other meeting places in your area. You will need a room which will hold up to 80 people for a meeting and accommodation overnight for up to 40. Make sure that you obtain prices for all the costs listed in Activity 1. If you are unable to spare the time to research this you will find some guidelines on prices in the table below. If at all possible, however, you should obtain some local prices for comparison. |

The Town Hotel

Tariff and Price List

	Per person
Single room per night (bath), b & b	£36.75
Twin room per night, b & b	£34.00
Double room per night, b & b	£32.50
Single room per night (shower), b & b	£29.80
Luncheon	£5.90
Dinner	£7.80
Tea and biscuits	£0.45
Coffee and biscuits	£0.65
Wine per glass	£0.95
Conference room per session (morning, afternoon or evening)	£78.00

The conference room can accommodate up to one hundred people, each person seated with a desk space and clear view of the speaker's platform.

Audio-visual aid facilities available on request (all prices are quoted per session):

Film project	£15.00
O.H.P.	£10.00
White board	£5.00
Video recorder and T.V.	£10.00

You should by now have a comprehensive list of all the costs of the conference. Those costs not identified on the list above should be fairly simple to estimate, so you should now make sure that you have all the figures which you need.

As soon as you have done this you should label each cost as *fixed* or *variable*.

In the context of Activity 2 a **fixed cost** is one which will be the same, regardless of how many delegates attend the conference. A **variable cost** is one which will increase proportionally as more people attend. In other words, the unit cost (the cost per delegate) of a variable cost stays the same regardless of the number of delegates, whereas the more people who attend, the more thinly the fixed costs are spread, and so the lower the fixed cost per delegate.

You should have decided that the fixed costs of the conference would be items such as the lecturers' fees, hire of room and equipment. Variable costs would be those such as meals, refreshments and stationery, where the organizers can just pay for enough to cover the number of delegates attending the conference.

| **Activity 3** | The best estimate your manager can give you is that not more than 100 people will be interested in attending the conference and, since this is the maximum capacity of the room in the Town Hotel, you decide to set a limit of 100 on the tickets for sale. |

The conference fee will cover two complete days for non-residents. Anybody staying in the hotel overnight will be billed separately for dinner, bed and breakfast. Lecturers for this type of conference will expect to receive a fee of £50–£70 per day, depending on their status and expertise in the subject matter.

Your next job is to decide on a possible price and to establish a break-even point. Calculate a price for the conference in the form shown at the top of the next page:

	Per Delegate £
Two luncheons	
Morning coffee × 2	
Afternoon tea × 2	
etc.	
	....
Total variable cost per delegate	
times expected numbers	
Total variable costs	....
Fixed Costs	
Room Hire	
Lecturer's fees	
etc.	....
Total fixed costs	....
Total costs	....
Add desired 25% profit mark-up	....
Required revenue	
divided by 80 (expected number of delegates)	....
Minimum charge per delegate	
(rounded up to nearest £5)	....

Your answer for the conference price should be around £30.00, depending on what costs and prices you use.

Activity 4

Since you are uncertain about how many places you will be able to sell, you should now check on the effects of changes in sales or prices by drawing a break-even chart. You should go about this in the following stages (if you have already studied Block 6, this activity should be quite easy for you):

a We have already stated that the maximum number of delegates will be 100. The maximum revenue will therefore be 100 times the conference fee. This enables you to decide on the scale for each axis of the break-even chart. Having done this you should decide how to fit your graph onto the graph paper, and the sales line can then be drawn by connecting the origin of the graph to the point representing the maximum number of delegates, using a straight line.

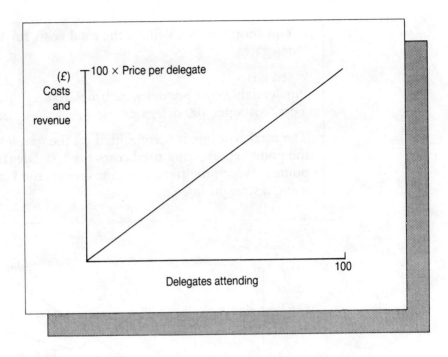

Revenue and
attendance.

b The next stage is to draw the line representing total
fixed costs as calculated in Activity 3. Since these costs
remain the same regardless of the number of delegates,
they will be represented by a horizontal line at the
appropriate point on the scale of revenue and costs.

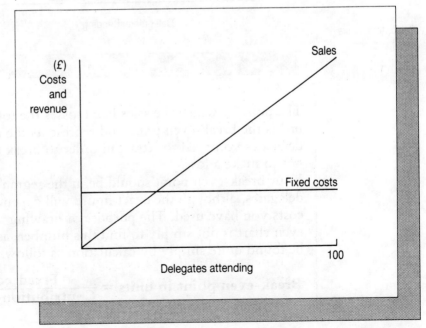

Sales and total
fixed costs.

c You should now calculate the total costs for 100
delegates.

Fixed costs   ....
Plus variable cost per delegate times 100   ....
Total costs per 100 delegates   ....

The total cost line is then plotted on the graph by joining
the point representing total costs for 100 delegates to the
point at which the fixed cost line crosses the vertical axis,
using a straight line.

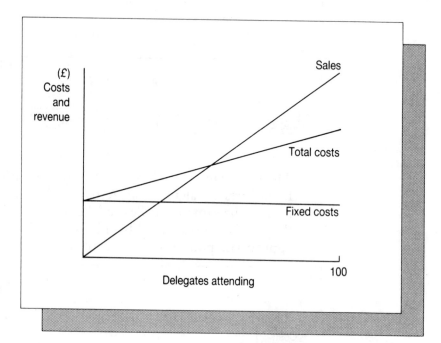

Sales, total costs
and fixed costs.

The point at which the sales line crosses the total cost
line is the break-even point and represents the number of
delegates you need to attract in order to break even, i.e.
not to make a loss.
Your break-even point should be in the region of 50
delegates, although the exact figure will depend on the
costs you have used. The purpose of drawing a break-
even chart is not simply to find this number, as this can
be found quite simply by calculation as follows:

$$\textbf{Break-even point in units} = \frac{\textbf{Fixed costs}}{\textbf{Contribution per unit}}$$

where

$$\text{Contribution per unit} = \text{Selling price per unit} \quad less \quad \text{Variable cost per unit}$$

Check your chart by trying the above calculation.

Activity 5

One of the more important reasons for drawing a chart is to be able to see the effects of changes in the variables quickly and simply.

Using the chart you have already drawn, draw lines which enable you to judge the effects of the following on the break-even point:
a a 10% increase in the selling price,
b a 10% fall in the selling price,
c an increase of £100 in the fixed costs,
d a decrease of £100 in the fixed costs,
e an increase of £2 per delegate in the variable costs,
f a decrease of £2 per delegate in the variable costs,
g sponsorship of the event by a local office supplies company; the terms are that they will pay you £150 to advertise on all the conference literature.

You should find that the effects of these changes would be as follows:

a A rise in the selling price will increase the contribution made by each unit. Consequently the number of delegates needed to break even will fall when the selling price rises.
b A fall in the selling price will reduce the contribution made by each unit. If this happens you will need more delegates before you break even, and this rise in the break-even point should show on the chart.
c If fixed costs rise by £100 then total costs at any given level of activity also increase by £100. The result of this is to raise the number of delegates needed to break even.
d With a lower level of fixed costs, total costs also fall at each level of activity, and thus the conference will break even with fewer delegates.
e An increase in costs for each delegate will reduce the contribution per delegate and thus raise the break-even point.
f If variable costs for each delegate are reduced, then fewer delegates will be needed to break even.

g The effect of a lump sum sponsorship for the conference would be the same as a reduction in fixed costs. You could assume that the sponsorship money is being used to pay some of these fixed costs, and thus that the net amount to be covered is reduced. The result of this is that the number of delegates needed to cover these fixed costs is reduced and so the break-even point is lower. You might like to consider what difference it would make if the sponsorship had been in terms of a sum for each delegate attending.

In all of the above cases, the amount and proportion of the rise or fall in break-even point depends on the figures you have used for the conference estimates in the first place.

Activity 6	Imagine now that the conference has taken place and that you sold 93 tickets. You have already decided on the charge for the conference alone and 35 delegates also chose to stay overnight at the hotel, 20 staying in single rooms with bath and 15 in single rooms with shower. They all had dinner in the restaurant. They then paid you for these facilities plus a 5% administration charge.

Draw up an accounting statement to show the results of the conference in as much detail as possible. |

Block 9
Financial Decisions and Large Capital Items

Personal finance

When considering personal finance, it is convenient to think in different scales. Personal expenditure might be divided into three separate categories:

A out-of-pocket expenditure which one makes day by day,
B larger expenses which may be regular or occasional, but which all cost less than about one week's income,
C expenditure on large items costing significantly more than one week's income.

Activity 1	List the type of item of personal finance which might fall into each of the above categories.

For Category A you have probably listed items such as bus fares, snacks and refreshments, newspapers, stationery, and other items costing little.

Category B includes items of regular household expenditure, such as rent, fuel, clothes, and household goods. It might also include small items which would nevertheless be used for some time, such as a hairbrush, a saucepan or a screwdriver: these are not large enough to be regarded as capital items, since their cost will be absorbed in a single week of the household budget.

Items included in Category C, such as cars, electrical goods, furniture, or even houses, will count as **capital items**. This implies that they will last for some time, that they cost a significant proportion of one's income, and that one will not buy them very often. Consequently the decision relating to paying for such an item is complicated and requires special techniques. While most of us will not spend much time considering whether or not to buy a cup of tea in the canteen, or a newspaper in the newsagent's shop, we would have to examine very carefully all aspects of purchasing a car or a hi-fi system. We have already explored the advantages and disadvantages of various methods of financing such a purchase in Block 1, and we shall now examine one special technique for deciding on the best method of payment.

Activity 2 | Imagine for a moment that you are offered a gift of £100. The terms of the offer are that you shall not be allowed to spend the money for one year, but that you may either receive it now or have a guarantee to receive it in one year's time. Which would you choose and why?

In Activity 2 you probably chose to receive the £100 now on the grounds that you could make a safe investment of the cash in something like a bank savings account, and your gift would be worth more by the time you were able to spend it. How much more would depend on the rate of interest at the time. If, for example, the rate of interest were 12% per annum then you would have £112 to spend when the year was up. This introduces a term which accountants and managers use to describe the value of cash receivable at some time in the future: they would say that the **present value** of £112 receivable one year from now, given an interest rate of 12%, is £100. Similarly, if the money were not receivable for two years, the £112 could be reinvested for a second year and thus grow to 112% of £112, i.e. £125.44. In this case we would say that the present value of £125.44 receivable two years from now, with a prevailing rate of interest of 12%, is £100. This technique recognizes the fact that money has a time value in that the sooner it is received the more it is worth to an individual or organization.

It is possible to draw up a table of factors which enables us to calculate the present value of any amount at various rates of interest, and such a table is shown opposite.

The relevance of the concept of present value is that, in buying a large item, it may not be necessary to pay cash for it immediately.

Present Value Discount Factors

Years	1%	2%	3%	4%	5%	6%	7%	8%	9%	10%
1	·9901	·9804	·9709	·9615	·9524	·9434	·9346	·9259	·9174	·9091
2	·9803	·9612	·9426	·9246	·9070	·8900	·8734	·8573	·8417	·8264
3	·9706	·9423	·9151	·8890	·8638	·8396	·8163	·7938	·7722	·7513
4	·9610	·9238	·8885	·8548	·8227	·7921	·7629	·7350	·7084	·6830
5	·9515	·9057	·8626	·8219	·7835	·7473	·7130	·6806	·6499	·6209
6	·9420	·8880	·8375	·7903	·7462	·7050	·6663	·6302	·5963	·5645
7	·9327	·8706	·8131	·7599	·7107	·6651	·6227	·5835	·5470	·5132
8	·9235	·8535	·7894	·7307	·6768	·6274	·5820	·5403	·5019	·4665
9	·9143	·8368	·7664	·7026	·6446	·5919	·5439	·5002	·4604	·4241
10	·9053	·8203	·7441	·6756	·6139	·5584	·5083	·4632	·4224	·3855
11	·8963	·8043	·7224	·6496	·5847	·5268	·4751	·4289	·3875	·3805
12	·8874	·7885	·7014	·6246	·5568	·4970	·4440	·3971	·3555	·3186
13	·8787	·7730	·6810	·6006	·5303	·4688	·4150	·3677	·3262	·2897
14	·8700	·7579	·6611	·5775	·5051	·4423	·3878	·3405	·2995	·2633
15	·8613	·7430	·6419	·5553	·4810	·4173	·3624	·3152	·2745	·2394
16	·8528	·7284	·6232	·5339	·4581	·3936	·3387	·2919	·2519	·2176
17	·8444	·7142	·6050	·5134	·4363	·3714	·3166	·2703	·2311	·1978
18	·8360	·7002	·5874	·4936	·4155	·3503	·2959	·2502	·2120	·1799
19	·8277	·6864	·5703	·4746	·3957	·3305	·2765	·2317	·1945	·1635
20	·8195	·6730	·5537	·4564	·3769	·3118	·2584	·2145	·1784	·1486

Years	11%	12%	13%	14%	15%	16%	17%	18%	19%	20%
1	·9009	·8929	·8850	·8772	·8696	·8621	·8547	·8475	·8403	·8333
2	·8116	·7972	·7831	·7695	·7561	·7432	·7305	·7182	·7062	·6944
3	·7312	·7118	·6931	·6750	·6575	·6407	·6244	·6086	·5934	·5787
4	·6587	·6355	·6133	·5921	·5718	·5523	·5537	·5158	·4987	·4823
5	·5935	·5674	·5428	·5194	·4972	·4761	·4561	·4371	·4190	·4019
6	·5346	·5066	·4803	·4556	·4323	·4104	·3898	·3704	·3521	·3349
7	·4817	·4523	·4251	·3996	·3759	·3538	·3332	·3139	·2959	·2791
8	·4339	·4039	·3762	·3506	·3269	·3050	·2848	·2660	·2487	·2326
9	·3909	·3606	·3329	·3075	·2843	·2630	·2434	·2255	·2090	·1938
10	·3522	·3220	·2946	·2679	·2472	·2267	·2080	·1911	·1756	·1615
11	·3173	·2875	·2607	·2366	·2149	·1954	·1778	·1619	·1476	·1346
12	·2855	·2567	·2307	·2076	·1869	·1685	·1520	·1372	·1240	·1122
13	·2575	·2292	·2042	·1821	·1625	·1452	·1299	·1163	·1042	·0935
14	·2320	·2046	·1807	·1597	·1413	·1252	·1110	·0985	·0876	·0779
15	·2090	·1827	·1599	·1401	·1229	·1079	·0949	·0835	·0736	·0649
16	·1883	·1631	·1415	·1229	·1069	·0930	·0811	·0708	·0618	·0541
17	·1696	·1456	·1252	·1078	·0929	·0802	·0693	·0600	·0520	·0451
18	·1528	·1300	·1108	·0946	·0808	·0691	·0592	·0508	·0437	·0376
19	·1377	·1161	·0981	·0829	·0703	·0596	·0506	·0431	·0367	·0313
20	·1240	·1031	·0868	·0728	·0611	·0514	·0433	·0365	·0308	·0261

Activity 3	Suppose that you are in the process of buying a television set. The shop offers terms of payment as follows: a *Cash price* £168, b *Purchase on credit* £84 deposit and a further payment of £84 in one year from now, c *Purchase on credit* £42 deposit plus three half-yearly payments of £42, d *Purchase on credit* £42 deposit plus three quarterly payments of £42. Which method of payment would you choose and why?

In Activity 3, if you are considering primarily the financial factors, then you should have chosen the half-yearly hire purchase option. But how can we prove this?

Let us assume that the cost of borrowing (and by implication the rate of interest available on deposits, although these usually differ by a small amount) is 12%. If this were the case, and using the idea of present value which has been explained above, we may express each of the options in terms of present value. We would then choose the method which shows the lowest present value as this would represent the lowest cost option.

a Clearly the present value of the cash price of £168 payable now is £168. There is no need to apply any adjustment to this figure as the payment is due immediately.

b In the case of the next option, the same is clearly true of the deposit of £84, which is payable immediately and is therefore already in present value terms. The payment in one year's time, however, should be adjusted by the appropriate discount factor. Reading from the table (p. 141) we find that the present value of £1 receivable or payable one year from now is £0.8929. Therefore the present value of the £84 payment in one year is

$$84 \times £0.8929 = £75.00.$$

The total present value of the cost of this option is therefore

$$£84.00 + £75.00 = £159.$$

c The remaining two options offer further complications. The period between payments is no longer one year, and the requirement of a number of payments means that a more formal layout of the calculations is desirable.

Period	Payment	Discount factor (6%)	Present value (£)
0	42.00	1.0000	42.00
1	42.00	0.9434	39.62
2	42.00	0.8900	37.38
3	42.00	0.8396	35.26
Total present value of payments			£154.26

The 6% rate has been chosen as the half-yearly equivalent of a 12% per annum or yearly rate. This does assume that a deposit account can be found which pays interest six-monthly, a not unreasonable assumption but one that should be used with care if the period between payments is as little as one month.

d Using the same method as above we can now calculate the total present value of payments for the quarterly option.

Period	Payment	Discount factor (6%)	Present value (£)
0	42.00	1.0000	42.00
1	42.00	0.9709	40.78
2	42.00	0.7426	39.59
3	42.00	0.9151	48.43
Total present value of payments			£160.80

The 3% rate has been chosen as the quarterly equivalent of a 12% per annum or yearly rate. This does assume that a deposit account can be found which pays interest quarterly, a slightly unreasonable assumption, and one that should be used with even greater care if the period between payments is as little as one month.

You will see therefore that the option of paying at six-monthly intervals has the lowest present value and is therefore the logical choice from a financial point of view. However, when making a decision such as this, you may wish to take into account other factors. Some people do not like to owe money and would therefore prefer to pay cash immediately. The method also assumes that some real alternative use will be made of the money for later instalments, and you may consider the effort of investing the cash in a deposit account too great for such a small return. The discount factor has nothing to do with inflation, but should there be inflation during the period there is a further benefit in delaying payment. If your income has risen because of inflation before later payments, then the proportion of income represented by each payment declines and the payment is therefore met by less work on your part.

| *Activity 4* | List all the other factors you would take into account when making your decision on the method of acquiring the use of the television set mentioned in Activity 3. |

Considerations other than present value when deciding on method of payment might include the following factors:

a a personal preference for paying cash rather than having hire–purchase debts,

b the availability of cash at the time you want to acquire use of the asset,

c your expectations regarding how much you might be earning when further payments are due,

d any conditions of the H.P. agreement requiring insurance of the set which would involve further cost,

e arrangements for servicing and repairs.

Both in this case and in the purchases of large items which we examined in Block 1, many factors will be taken into account when making such a choice. You should not imagine that this kind of technique provides a hard-and-fast rule for making decisions, or that it is a rule which must be followed at all times. Financial factors interact with other considerations and provide just one method of judging the reasons for making a particular decision.

Organizational finance

In much the same way as it is convenient to think of personal expenditure as falling into three categories, many organizations classify expenditure according to the nature of what is being bought. Normal everyday expenditure on goods for resale, materials for manufacture, wages, and other running expenses are known as **revenue expenditure**. The purchase of items which are to be used for some time within the organization for the purpose of generating profits, or to pursue the normal business of the organization, is known as **capital expenditure**. In this block we are concerned with the way in which organizations justify large items of capital expenditure, or the use of funds on projects which will generate revenue or make savings in costs. Making plans for the purchase of fixed assets is known as **capital budgeting**. In the area of capital budgeting, it is normal for organizations to set limits below which managers can spend without seeking special authority. For larger projects, or items of capital expenditure, a complete examination of expected financial effects will be necessary. When this is the case, a number of considerations will be taken into account, and a number of specific techniques are available for clarifying the financial situation.

There are two distinct situations which may face an organization about to make capital expenditure. Firstly, having already decided on the need for a particular item of expenditure, such as the replacement of a machine, the organization will be seeking the model and method of purchase which is financially most favourable. Secondly, an organization normally has limited funds and needs to choose the more financially favourable out of a number of competing projects. Similar techniques are used to make decisions in each of these cases and we shall now examine these.

Activity 5	Let us first take a simple example and examine some of the factors which an organization would consider when making a decision.
	The MLK Manufacturing Company is considering the purchase of a machine which manufactures paperclips. This will complement its increasing involvement in the field of stationery and office equipment. The financial

details associated with this project are as follows:
a The cost of purchasing the machine is £7 600 and it is
  expected to last for four years.
b It will take the firm some time to build up its market
  for paperclips and the returns will vary from one year
  to the next. The predicted cash flow generated over the
  life of the machine, net of all direct material and labour
  costs, and machine repairs and servicing is

Year	£
1	2 000
2	2 300
3	2 900
4	2 700

Make notes and calculations which you could use when
talking to a manager of the organization about whether
or not to buy the machine. List also any questions which
you would ask in order to make a decision from an
informed standpoint.

Your notes should include both financial and other
considerations.

Some of the points you may have included in your own lists
for Activity 4 are set out below.
1 How confident is the firm about the estimates of costs and
  income which it has made?
2 What basis does the firm use when making a decision on
  major capital expenditure?
3 What is the current rate of interest or cost of capital for the
  firm?
4 What is the policy on depreciation of machinery?
5 What effects would the purchase of the machine have on
  the workforce? Does the manpower exist to operate the
  machine or would somebody new have to be trained or
  somebody be newly employed?
6 Would it be appropriate to charge depreciation equally over
  the four years, making it £1 900 each year? Should your
  decision on depreciation affect the overall situation at all?

Clearly some systematic approach is needed to this type of
decision: organizations will be making such decisions
frequently. We shall now examine different techniques which
provide us with guidance on the financial aspects of the
decision.

The payback period

One reason for buying a machine is to generate cash income. An organization may therefore choose to assess how long it will take for the original investment to be repaid by the cash which it generates. This period of time is then known as the **payback period**.

The payback period is calculated quite simply. In our example the MLK Manufacturing Company is planning for expenditure of £7 600 and expecting this to generate cash flows of

Year	£
1	2 000
2	2 300
3	2 900
4	2 700

By the end of Year 1 therefore the project has brought in £2 000. By the end of Year 2 the following total has been produced:

$$(£2 000 + £2 300 = £4 300.)$$

In Year 3 a further £2 900 is generated making a total of £7 200 by the end of this period.

Since the cost of the project was £7 600 it should now be clear to you that the payback point occurs at some time during the fourth year. A further £400 (cost *less* cash generated so far, or £7 600 − £7 200) is needed. Assuming that the flow of cash is steady through the year the payback period occurs after

$$\frac{400}{2 700} = 0.148 \text{ of the year.}$$

You can convert this into months, by multiplying by 12, to find that the payback period occurs after 1.8 months of Year 4.

The company may have a policy which states that any project must pay back in three years, and if this were the case the purchase of the paperclip machine would be turned down. Alternatively, if the machine is just one of a number of possible projects for the company, then they might choose the project with the shortest payback period. Many organizations use this method simply as a preliminary means of sifting out investments with a very long payback period. The method is simple and quick, and therefore provides an easy way of comparing possible investments. The great disadvantage of the payback period as a sole means of ranking and choosing projects is that all returns after the payback point are ignored. To follow a choice made by this method without further examination may therefore lead organizations to ignore projects which produce returns for long periods of time.

The main lesson of this is that financial methods should be used as indicators only, to be examined together with all other factors, and not to be followed in an unquestioning way.

The average rate of return

An alternative way of assessing an investment is to look at the potential profits to be earned from the project. As we have previously discovered, the profit from a project or enterprise is not the same as the cash flow which it generates. Before an acceptable profit figure can be expressed, a depreciation charge for the capital equipment must be made. In our example it has been suggested that the machine might be depreciated on a straight line basis, that is to say by charging £1900 each year against profits. If this is so then the profit in each year may be found by deducting £1900 from the predicted annual cash flow in each case.

Year	Cash flow £	Depreciation £	Profit £
1	2 000	1 900	100
2	2 300	1 900	400
3	2 900	1 900	1 000
4	2 700	1 900	800
		Total profit	2 300

The average profit per annum is a simple calculation once the total profit is known. Simply divide the total profits by the number of years:

$$\frac{£2\,300}{4} = £575 \text{ per annum.}$$

A very common way to express the profits of an organization is to compare them with the amount invested to produce those profits. This measure is very popular amongst business people because it can be easily compared with the return produced by investing the money elsewhere, such as in a deposit account where risk is at a minimum. In the case of the purchase of machinery or other fixed assets, the amount invested declines as the book value of the asset declines. When the expenditure is first made the firm has £7 600 invested in the project. At the end of the project no capital is invested in the project. On average, therefore, the capital employed, or tied up, in the project is half of the original investment. The result of this is that the average amount invested may be found as follows:

$$\frac{\text{Initial cost less scrap value}}{2} = \frac{£7\,600 - 0}{2} = £3\,800.$$

If we now wish to assess the average rate of return on the project we simply express the average profit as a percentage of the average capital employed or amount invested:

$$\frac{£575 \times 100}{£3\,800} = 15.1\%.$$

This profit could then be compared with the return on other investments being made by the organization and, if considered satisfactory, the project would be undertaken. Once again there are advantages in this system of assessing projects, but there are also problems. The choice of a method of depreciation may well be affected by considerations which have nothing to do with the project under consideration, such as tax advantages. If this is the case then decisions may be made for the wrong reasons. More important than this, however, is the fact that the method treats returns which are received in the near future in the same way as those predicted for the distant future. This ignores the time value of money related to the possibility of making secure investments at compound rates of interest. It also ignores the fact that forecasts for later periods are less reliable.

It may not be entirely appropriate therefore to use this form of the return on capital employed ratio, which is so useful when assessing the overall performance of an organization, to assess individual projects. On the other hand, many projects produce a fairly even cash flow, thus making the time value of money less relevant. If this is the case, then a manager may choose to use the average rate of return as an indicator which closely parallels his or her assessments of performance in the organization as a whole. It should also be noted that the financial return on a project is just one factor to be taken into account when making an investment decision. Many other aspects of the decision should be considered by a manager and we shall examine these in more detail at the end of this block.

Following the introduction to this block which examined the technique of discounting in relation to certain aspects of personal finance, you have probably guessed by now that we shall be describing discounting methods used to assess investment projects for organizations.

Discounted cash flow techniques

We have already examined the meaning of the term *present value*, and it should be clear to you that the manager making a decision on the investment in the paper–clip machine in our example will be interested in discovering the present value of the returns from the project. We may calculate this quite easily once we have been told that for the MLK Manufacturing Company, at the time in question, the **cost of capital** is 15% per annum.

This figure of cost of capital is usually estimated as the average cost to borrow the money for the original investment. It is not relevant whether or not the organization plans actually to borrow the cash since, if it is supplying its own, there is an opportunity cost of interest foregone by not investing the money in a secure deposit account at low risk.

To calculate the present value of the cash flows produced by the paper–clip machine, we proceed as follows:

Year	Cash flow	15% Discount factor	Present value
	£		£
1	2 000	0.8696	1739.20
2	2 300	0.7561	1739.03
3	2 900	0.6575	1906.75
4	2 700	0.5718	1543.86
Total present value of returns			6928.84

Remember that the project has cost the organization £7 600 to undertake. As the £7 600 must be spent at the start of the project, it is by definition already in present value terms and is greater than the present value of the returns produced by the investment. The difference between these figures is known as the **net present value** (NPV) of the project.

Two conclusions may be drawn from this calculation: firstly, that because the return is less than the investment, the firm will not proceed with the project. If the organization can obtain a 15% return by investing the money in a virtually risk-free manner, it will gain more financially than it would by operating the paper-clip machine. This leads us directly to the second conclusion: that the investment in this machine produces less than a 15% return.

Had the net present value of the project been positive (the present value of returns exceeding original investment), we would conclude that the return from the investment was greater than 15%.

---

original investment larger than present value of returns
▽
net present value negative
▽
percentage return of discount factor is not achieved

---

original investment smaller than present value of returns
▽
net present value positive
▽
project exceeds percentage return of discount factor

---

original investment equal to discount factor
▽
net present value zero
▽
return on project is exactly percentage of discount factor

The internal rate of return

We have discovered above that the paper–clip project makes less than 15% return, but can we say what percentage return it does produce in terms of present value? For this we must find a percentage discount which produces a total present value equal to the original investment, that is to say a rate which produces a net present value of zero. Since we know it to be less than 15% our next move is to try a lower discount factor, such as 10%.

Year	Cash flow	10% Discount factor	Present value
	£		£
1	2 000	0.9091	1818.20
2	2 300	0.8264	1900.72
3	2 900	0.7513	2178.77
4	2 700	0.6830	1844.10
Total present value of returns			7669.07

Net present value of returns = £7669.07 *less* £7600 = **£69.07**

The net present value of the project is now positive (the present value of the returns exceeds the cost) so we can see that the project produces more than 10% return. Will it produce as much as 12%?

Year	Cash flow	12% Discount factor	Present value
	£		£
1	2 000	0.8929	1785.80
2	2 300	0.7972	1833.56
3	2 900	0.7118	2064.22
4	2 700	0.6355	1715.85
Total present value of returns			7399.43

Net present value = £7399.43 *less* £7600 = **(£200.57)**

Note: it is an accounting convention that figures in brackets have a negative value.

The project clearly does not make 12% as the present value of the returns is less than the cost. We are now in a position to say, however, that it does produce between 10% and 12% return. We can estimate the precise return as follows:

$$\text{Internal rate of return} = 10\% + \left(\frac{69.07}{69.07 + 200.57} \times 2\%\right) = 10.51\%.$$

Most of the figures in this calculation are easily traced in the earlier part of the example. The 10% is the lower percentage which produced a positive net present value; the £69.07 is the net present value produced when using this lower percentage. The £69.07 and £200.57 is the range of values for the net present value produced when the two percentages, one either side of the internal rate of return, have been tried. The 2% is the difference between the 12% and the 10% in the trial and error stage of the process. This process is known as **interpolation** and is a simplified arithmetic method of estimating the precise rate of return. It makes certain mathematical assumptions which in fact mean that the rate produced by this method is slightly imprecise, but it is quite accurate enough for most purposes. One should however never use a gap of more than 2% as the difference between the trial and error attempts at finding a net present value of zero, as the potential error then becomes more significant. The mathematics underlying this technique are outside the scope of this course and are rather complex. You would be well advised, therefore, to concentrate on the fairly simple arithmetic steps needed to calculate the right answer.

| *Activity 6* | A company is considering investing in two possible projects. It cannot afford to carry out both projects, but you are asked to consider which project will be best for the company on financial grounds. |

	Project A	Project B
	£	£
Initial investment	100 000	100 000
Net cash savings		
Year 1	5 000	60 000
Year 2	20 000	40 000
Year 3	100 000	100 000
Year 4	10 000	5 000

> *Note:* Savings represent a reduction in cash outflows and may therefore be treated as a positive cash flow.
>
> *a* If the company requires a return of 14%, which project would be preferable?
>
> *b* What is the internal rate of return for the project which you have chosen?

Is the discounted cash flow method then the best or only way to evaluate projects from a financial point of view? It has the advantage that it produces a simple comparison of expenditure and returns all in the same dimension, or else if the internal rate of return is calculated, a direct comparison with rates of interest available elsewhere. This should enable the business manager to follow a simple set of rules regarding rates of return when selecting projects. The problems arise however in that this method relies heavily on predictions and projections. All cash flows must be estimated and included, and the accuracy of estimates relating to periods in the distant future must be open to question. The method also works on the assumption of a definable and consistent rate of interest as the cost of capital, but it may be extremely difficult, or simply not possible, to set a realistic rate of interest. If one allows for inflation, with different cash flows at different rates, the calculations also become extremely complicated.

We must also take careful note that, like other methods, this method only gives us an indication of financial aspects of the decision. Any manager must consider the investment in the light of the organization as a whole, and non-financial considerations may well be more important in many cases.

A comparison of the different methods

Before we look at a realistic example of an investment decision, let us consider all the methods together.

Payback period
Advantages
Quick and easy
Concentrates on early cash flow
Disadvantages
Ignores returns beyond payback date
Ignores time value of money
Ignores scrap value

Average rate of return

Advantages

Expresses rate in terms of profit

Produces figure comparable with overall organizational
  performance measurement

Disadvantages

Relies on subjective choice of depreciation method

Ignores time value of money

Requires estimates of returns in the distant future

Discounted cash flow techniques

Advantages

Take account of time value of money

Produce a measure to compare with cost of capital or prevailing
  rate of interest

Disadvantages

Complex calculations

Requires estimates of returns in the distant future

| Activity 7 | A local company is considering buying a new machine for £11 000 which it estimates will save £2 800 in cash operating costs for each of the next ten years. At the end of the ten years the machine is expected to have no scrap value.

The company requires a rate of return of 14% on its projects.

Prepare a report on the features you think the company should consider when evaluating the project and specifically calculate the net present value. |

| Activity 8 | The chairman of Club A is currently in negotiation with the chairman of Club B for the purchase of a star football player, Roy Pace.

Club B want £600 000 in cash for the player and Club A have offered £500 000 plus Tony Gamble who currently earns £15 000 per year with Club A.

The chairman and manager of Club A have entrusted the following features of this proposed deal: |

estimated useful life of Roy Pace   5 years
estimated sale value of Pace after 5 years   £20 000
estimated useful life of Gamble   5 years
estimated sale value of Gamble after 5 years   none

Current cost offer for Gamble from Club C   £500 000

Acceptable rate of return   10%

Other information:

	Pace's salary £	Extra gate receipts after Pace's arrival £	Extra costs of larger crowds £
Year 1	60 000	330 000	33 000
Year 2	70 000	300 000	30 000
Year 3	80 000	200 000	20 000
Year 4	80 000	100 000	10 000
Year 5	72 000	40 000	4 000

As the above information shows, it is very difficult to estimate the various facts and features of a decision of this kind. No doubt some of the estimates are made with very little certainty of their being accurate. Nevertheless they need to be made. Do you think that Club A should buy Roy Pace?

Concluding comments

When deciding whether or not to undertake this type of project, an organization should always consider the financial position. The final decision, however, will depend on a number of factors and not solely the financial situation. Management should establish their own priorities for the types of activity to be undertaken by an organization and then decide on the costs which they are willing to bear for each activity. Companies in the private sector often undertake a variety of activities, some more profitable than others. Some capital expenditure is made for the benefit of staff welfare or public relations even if it cannot be justified in purely financial terms. You should be aware, therefore, that simply arriving at a financial 'answer' only provides a guideline for management and should not be the only basis for decisions.

Block 10
Finance and Non-trading Organizations

Previous blocks have dealt with finance as a resource for either individuals or businesses that hope to generate a profit. But some organizations are not set up to create profits: they are designed to provide a service.

This does not mean however that finance is unimportant in such organizations. These organizations have to be careful to use their finance effectively so that the service they provide will be as full and beneficial as possible. What sorts of organization are in this category? Below are some examples:

Sports clubs	Local football clubs, cricket clubs, bowls clubs, rugby clubs, tennis clubs, etc.
Social clubs	Drama societies, gardening clubs, etc.
Other associations	Tenant associations, professional societies for accountants and lawyers, etc.

Activity 1 List organizations, in addition to those mentioned above, that provide a service rather than aim to make a profit.

Activity 2 List the ways you think the organizations you have listed for Activity 1 could raise revenue or income.

To be able to offer facilities or services, non-trading organizations must raise revenue. The method used will depend on the type of organization. Typical sorts of methods are annual subscriptions, dances, social events, operating a bar, providing a 'gaming' or 'video machine' and sponsorship.

Activity 3 List the factors you think might influence an organization or individual considering sponsoring a club, organization or event.

Accounting records

All organizations need to keep records of the transactions they undertake. Block 4, which deals with accounting records and financial statements, illustrates statements produced by businesses: profit and loss accounts, and balance sheets.

Organizations whose purpose is not to make a profit still need to report to members or subscribers on the financial state of the organization. This means that some sort of record keeping is necessary. For non-trading organizations, as for all organizations, the problem is what sort of records to keep. It is a very useful rule to follow that the records kept should be designed to suit the sort of final reports that need to be produced. For example, in the case of a company's profit and loss account, it could only be produced if records are maintained of sales revenue, costs incurred, and so on. A balance sheet is really only a statement showing the assets owned and the liabilities of a business at a particular point in time, usually the end of the financial year. Again, without initial records of assets purchased, loans received and cash in hand, this statement could not be produced.

Non-profit-making organizations, such as the ones you may have listed for Activity 1, will no doubt keep records in a different way from large businesses. The sort of accounting statements they need to prepare at the end of accounting periods will be different, and so will the sort of transactions they carry out.

Income, from whatever source, needs to be recorded and expenditure similarly recorded. If this is done, an **income and expenditure account** can be produced, effectively listing areas where income has been made and expenses incurred. Perhaps for a sports club the following income analysis would be required:

				Ticket Sales		
Date	Subscriptions	Match fees	Raffle	Barbecue	Dance	Total

Income account for a club.

If expenditure is analysed in a similar fashion, it is a simple job to extract totals at the end of a year to produce statements that show an analysis of income and expenditure. Of equal importance to income and expenditure is the idea of maintaining **control**. Treasurers are usually appointed by these organizations to keep records; they have to report to committees and to members and need to keep control over transactions. If records are kept of each and every transaction, this makes control possible.

In a sports club, expenditure would perhaps be analysed in the following way:

Date	Ticket printing	Rent for ground	Playing equipment	Insurance	Total

Expenditure account for a club.

Activity 4 Select a local sports or social organization, e.g. the students union or any local group, and see if you can find out how they keep records of transactions. Discuss with other students the reasons for any differences in the sort of records they keep.

Activity 5 Have a careful look at the final accounts that follow of a sports and social club. The accounts consist of an income and expenditure account, a bar trading and profit and loss account, and a balance sheet. Compare these accounts with the statements produced by profit-orientated businesses, as discussed in Block 4. Look for any differences in,
a style of presentation,
b content.

SUNRISE SPORTS CLUB

Bar Trading and Profit and Loss Account for the year ended 30 September, 1986

	£	£
Bar takings (excluding Value Added Tax)		12395
Beers, wines, spirits and sundries		
Opening stock	831	
Purchases	8323	
	9154	
Closing stock	787	
Costs of Goods Sold (excluding Value Added Tax)		8367
Gross Profit		4028 (32.49%)
Gaming maching receipts		831
Locker rents		61
		4920
Stewards' salary, state contributions, and casual help	3427	
Gaming machine operating expenses	540	
Repairs & renewals, & sundry expenses	128	
Depreciation	217	4312
Net Profit for the year		608

SUNRISE SPORTS CLUB

Income and Expenditure Account for the year ended 30 September, 1986

Income		£	
Subscriptions (less levies paid)		19 602	
Fees		2 791	
Net profit as shown by Bar Account		608	
Amounts received from 100 Club		1 312	
Sundry income		243	
Donation		250	
Bank interest received		526	
		25 332	
Expenditure			
Sports ground			
Groundsman and casual labour	5 822		
Materials for maintenance & sundry expenses	1 907	7 729	
Tractors & machinery			
Fuel	807		
Repairs and maintenance	3 420	4 227	
Club house			
Heating and lighting	1 904		
Water charges	477		
Telephone charges (less coin box receipts)	159		
Repairs and renewals	1 057		
Sundry expenses	880	4 477	
Rent		500	
Rates		1 901	
Administration			
Printing, stationery, adverts, postages and petty cash	419		
Insurance	742		
Accountancy charges	175		
Bank charges	115	1 451	
Finance			
Loan interest (Allied Breweries)	430		
Legal charges re repayment of loan	30		
Corporation tax	94		
Depreciation	866	1 420	
		21 705	
Excess of Income over Expenditure for the year		3 627	

A set of accounts
for a Sports Club.

SUNRISE SPORTS CLUB

Balance Sheet as at 30 September, 1986

	£	£
Fixed Assets		
As at 1 October 1985	26 269	
Improvements during the year	2 588	28 857
Club house		
As at 1 October 1985	29 116	
Improvements during the year	2 686	31 802
Bar fixtures & fittings, furniture and equipment		
As at 1 October 1985	964	
Additions during the year	1 211	
	2 175	
Less depreciation	217	1 958
Tractors & mowers		
As at 1 October 1985	8 663	
Less depreciation	866	7 797
		70 414
Current Assets		
Bar stocks	787	
Debtor (VAT repayment)	134	
Balance at bank	4 752	
Cash in hand	90	
	5 763	
Less Current Liabilities		
Sundry creditors	2 800	
Net Current Assets		2 963
Net Assets		73 377
Represented by		
Capital reserve		
Balance at 1 October 1985	33 918	
Add fees received during year	1 778	35 696
Revenue reserve		
Income and expenditure account		
balance at 1 October 1985	29 674	
Add excess of income over expenditure for the year	3 627	33 301
		68 997

Loans	£	£
Fine brewers		
Amount advanced during the year		2 100
Members as at 1 October 1985	2 730	
Less amounts repaid	750	1 980
Members bonds as at 1 October 1986		300
		73 377

I have prepared the above accounts from the records and information
supplied to me, without carrying out an audit, and in my opinion they
are in accordance herewith.

This particular social organization, a sports club, is fairly large. It has assets: its own ground and a club house that has a bar. Income comes from fees and subscriptions from members plus profit from the bar. Expenditure is on ground maintenance and on service charges such as electricity, water and roads for the club house, plus administrative and financial charges.

The treasurer will need to classify income and expenditure into appropriate categories when transactions take place, otherwise statements such as those above could not be prepared.

In the case of the Sunrise Sports Club, because the subscriptions are a very large amount, and represent a large percentage of the total income, a system will be necessary to ensure that all members pay match fees and annual subscriptions.

Activity 6	How do you think subscriptions will be dealt with in a club such as the Sunrise Sports Club? *a* Will invoices be sent out to members? *b* How will money received for subscriptions be dealt with? *c* What should the club do about ensuring that every member pays promptly?

Value Added Tax

The accounts for the Sunrise Sports Club include an item, 'Value Added Tax repayment', indicating that the club is owed an amount by the Customs and Excise Department for VAT.

Businesses are obliged to register for VAT if their turnover is above a certain level. They then charge their customers VAT on the goods and services they provide. Similarly their suppliers charge them VAT. Effectively then, any registered business or organization is both paying and being paid for VAT.

At the end of each three month period (quarter) a return has to be sent to the local Customs and Excise Department to account for these VAT transactions. The return will detail the VAT paid on purchases and also the VAT charged on sales or goods supplied. The amount owing to Customs and Excise will then be paid or, in the case of our illustration, a refund of VAT will be made.

VAT applies to all business, not just the kinds of non-trading organizations described in this block.

Activity 7 Collect information from your local Customs and Excise office, e.g. booklets or fact sheets, explaining how VAT works. Do not worry about the detail of the booklets but try to find out,

a the minimum turnover needed in order to be forced to register,

b what items might be exempt from VAT,

c the forms or returns that have to be made each quarter.

The Sports Club in the illustration will have had to keep VAT records on its purchases and income. Probably an extra 'column' has been added to the headings we have shown so that totals can be extracted readily for the quarterly VAT return, as in this extract from the cash book.

Date	Subscription	100 Club	Dances	Playing fees	Other	VAT	Total

Extract from a cash book.

Probably each of the headings in the cash book will be totals from separate records kept for each form of income. This may take the form of just a separate page in an analysed accounts book, obtainable from stationers, but perhaps, if the records are kept on computer, a separate file will detail all subscriptions, all income from the 100 Club, all donations, etc. A totalling exercise is then made much easier.

Software packages are generally available that are specially designed for this kind of use. They are designed to do a similar job to the analysed accounts books available from stationers, but they save the need to record manually income and expenditure. Instead, by typing in a code the item of income or expenditure is automatically analysed by its type so that totals can be extracted at the end of the accounting period.

Whilst thinking about computers and the available software for them for the recording of transactions for social clubs, you should think about the ways computers can help in keeping records and presenting information for all types of organizations.

| *Activity 8* | Write to computer manufacturers requesting information, or collect information from your college, on computer applications for recording financial transactions. Expect to find information on software packages that offer sales and purchase ledger information, wage and payroll information, and spreadsheets that help to display data in a helpful and fully analysed way. |

The important feature to remember, however, is not having knowledge and information about computers, but using computers yourself, so that you become familiar with the keyboards and the data and information that they can provide.

Block 11
Public Organizations

Introduction

The previous block dealt with the finance of those organizations often called *non-trading organizations*. They are structured to provide a service and, as we have seen, this service is often to members who form a club or society.

Public undertakings, such as the health service, libraries and education also provide a service, but such services are fundamental to the society we live in, and not a matter of individual choice. We mostly take for granted the provision of schools, colleges, doctors and dentists, but those activities have to be funded from somewhere. We all contribute to these services through taxes and rates.

Control needs to be carried out in these public organizations to make sure that funds are properly used. This block takes one service in particular, the National Health Service (NHS), and examines how it operates and how it accounts for the funds it uses. Other government services, either national or local, may operate differently, but this block will help to explain the different procedures that are followed compared with a privately owned business.

To some extent this block can be seen as a study of one particular branch of publicly funded operations. There are, of course, many others, but looking at the NHS as a base should provide an introduction for studies of other areas of locally or centrally funded operations. This block then becomes more of a case-study, in that it is concerned with a particular area of national funding, but general principles are shared with other nationalized activities.

The National Health Service

The NHS provides us with hospitals, an ambulance service, family doctors, dentists and clinics.

The National Health Service Structure

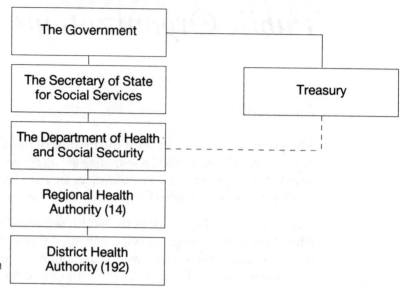

The National Health Service structure.

This simple chart shows how the health service is administered, and the relationship between local provision and the national government.

Finance

In 1982/83, the cost of running the National Health Service was £14 549 million. Almost 98% of the total cost of running the NHS comes from public funds. The other 2% is made up from income collected from patients, and others, for treatment and other services, e.g. treatment after road traffic accidents.

Parliament decides on the total sum of money to be spent on the NHS each year. Over 80% of the money spent on the NHS is subject to **cash limits**; this means that only a certain amount of money is available. Health Authorities must therefore only spend money within the limited cash available to them.

Spending on Family Practitioner Services (FPS), e.g. family doctors, immunization programmes, is judged to be **demand determined**. For example, when epidemics, such as whooping cough, occur there is an increase in demand on doctors and support services. Money has to be available to treat this kind of epidemic, so because of such circumstances Parliament cannot limit the amount available.

From 1 April 1985, the FPS has been funded directly by the Department of Health and Social Security.

Resource allocation

Once Parliament has decided on the total amount of money to be spent on the National Health Service, the Department of Health and Social Security (DHSS) is responsible for allocating money to the 14 Regional Health Authorities (RHAs).

In 1975 the Resource Allocation Working Party (RAWP) was set up to devise a method of making sure the money available was distributed evenly to RHAs in relation to population, structure of the population, level of illness, etc.

This involves setting a target level of expenditure for each region, based on the estimated demand for services. For example, a higher density of older people in a retirement area, such as Bournemouth, will require the allocation of more resources relating to the treatment of geriatric disorders.

RHAs receive three separate major allocations of money from the DHSS:

1 capital,
2 revenue,
3 joint finance.

The RHA then allocates the money available to the District Health Authorities (DHAs) in its region. This is done again on the basis of formulae produced by RAWP.

| *Activity 1* | Obtain the Financial Report for the District Health Authority in your area and answer the following questions:
a How many members sit on the District Health Authority and who appoints them?
b What services are provided to the community by the DHA?
c What is the population of the community?
d What percentage of the population is over 65?
e What is the total cash limits allocation to the DHA?
f What are the amounts specified for
    revenue?
    capital?
    joint funding? |

Health authority statutory accounts and statements

There is no statutory requirement for health authorities to publish a financial report. However, NHS treasurers have formed the Association for Healthcare Financial Management and have agreed to produce financial reports on a voluntary basis. These reports are available to the public, and copies can be examined in libraries and hospitals in the area served by the health authority.

However, Section 98 of the National Health Service Act, 1977, requires health authorities to produce accounts at the end of each financial year, for the period 1 April to 31 March each year.

Health authorities carry out their main accounting procedures and prepare their annual financial accounts and statements within a clear national framework. This is to facilitate comparisons between authorities, and for monitoring purposes by the DHSS and Parliament.

The Secretary of State for Social Services issues instructions and directions in Health Service Directions and Circulars concerning the form of accounts and supporting cost statements. There is therefore a nationally adopted form of accounts and supporting cost statements.

The following pages contain extracts from the reports and accounts issued by the Walsall District Health Authority.

Extracts from the reports and accounts of a district Health Authority.

Treasurer's Report

Introduction

In 1984/85 the cost of running Hospital, Community and Family Practitioner Services in Walsall totalled £202 for each resident or 55p a day. This booklet explains how these resources were spent and supplements the statutory financial statements required by the DHSS which the Authority is formally required to adopt.

Where the Money comes from:

The West Midlands Regional Health Authority is the largest of the fourteen English Regions and receives its funds from the Department of Health. In turn it allocates 'cash limits' to Districts which represent the maximum sum which may be spent on local health services. The total sum is divided into three separate categories:

Revenue – For paying salaries and other day to day running costs

Capital – For providing buildings and major pieces of equipment and vehicles.

Joint Funding – For the Local Authority and Health Authority to spend on schemes which compliment or relieve pressure on health services.

It is the responsibility of the District Health Authority to ensure that the services it provides are contained within the cash limit and that developments of service can be fully funded.

Flexibility exists within cash limits for revenue underspendings to be carried forward to the next financial year up to a level of 1%, whereas all overspendings must be charged against the following year's allocation. The same rules apply to capital except that the carryforward level for underspendings is 10%.

By agreement with the RHA transfers may be made between revenue and capital. From revenue to capital up to a maximum of 1% of the revenue cash limit and from capital to revenue up to a maximum of 10% of the capital cash limit.

Treasurer's Report

Financial Performance

Because of its recognised underfunding Walsall received a higher than average development addition from the West Midlands RHA in 1984/85 amounting to £935,000 or 2.8% added to balances brought forward from 1983/84 of £229,000. This strong opening position has provided a sound basis on which to implement a number of new services in the District which, together with a trend towards increased throughput, has resulted in a small revenue cash limit overspending of £48,000 for the year. The summary statement below highlights the final 'cash limit' position for each category of finance.

In terms of 'income' and 'expenditure' accounting, the revenue allocation shows an overspending of £24,000. This latter form of accounting is the approach adopted for local control where more sensitivity is required to ensure that expenditure and income is related to commitments and services actually used. A statement reconciling the two approaches is reproduced on page 12.

	Revenue £000	Capital £000	Joint Finance £000
Cash Limit	34,037	1,751	468
Charge against Cash Limit	34,085	1,757	468
Overspending	+48	+6	—

Looking Ahead

The District's commitment to improved efficiency is by no means new. The real savings achieved in 1984/85 are expected to be supplemented in 1985/86 and will lead to an extension of direct patient services. The process of competitive tendering begun in 1984 is now well underway along with the rigorous implementation of manpower targets and the creation of the General Management function.

The coming year will see increasing emphasis placed on the information needs of management and the computer technology necessary to provide that data. To this extent the District expects to implement the Patient Administration System, continue the development of the Manpower Management System and begin the first phase of Management Budgeting on the Acute Hospital site.

Treasurer's Report

In recent years the economic climate has resulted in some uncertainty in the levels of inflation coupled with the establishment of Pay Review bodies. Plans for the year ahead are therefore subject to adjustment depending on the levels of pay settlement and Government support to meet any excess costs over approved reserves.

Together with Phase IV of the District General Hospital the Regional Capital Programme for Walsall contains substantial new developments which will begin to alleviate the shortage of health care in Acute, Geriatric and Mental Illness services during the next five years. It is the Health Authority's intention to monitor very closely the construction programme and in due course the funding of these new services by the Region.

Acknowledgement

The changing emphasis brought about by the Griffiths recommendations from team management to personal accountability of individual professionals provides a challenge to all of us involved in Health Service administration.

I am pleased to acknowledge the increasing responsibility taken at Unit level on financial management matters and the continuing commitment shown by Budget Holders.

Once again I should like to acknowledge the continuing support of all my staff and the team effort which they have shown.

Roger Thompson
District Treasurer

July, 1985

Accounting Policies

General Principles

The principles adopted in the compilation and presentation of the 1984/85 statutory accounts are those laid down by the DHSS Statutory Financial Instructions and as recommended by the Association of Health Service Treasurer's.

Debtors and Creditors

The revenue transactions of the Authority are recorded on an income and expenditure basis. That is, all sums due to or from the Authority in the year of account are included, irrespective of whether the cash has actually been received or paid. Capital transactions are recorded on a cash basis.

Stock Valuation

Items held on the computerised stores system are valued at weighted average price. Other items are valued at actual cost prices on a First In First Out Basis (FIFO).

Depreciation

All hospitals and other buildings are government property. The NHS does not at present have a system of fixed assets accounting and therefore no reserve is made for depreciation.

Investments

The Authority maintains its cash balances at the lowest workable level in accordance with DHSS policy and statutorily these are not available for investment. Trust fund cash balances are available for investment and are shown in the Trust Fund Balance Sheet at cost value.

Audit

This booklet is based on the statutory accounts which are issued subject to audit in order to provide information as early as possible.

Source and Application of Funds—Revenue

	£000	£000
Source of Funds		
Revenue Cash Limit		34,037.0
Application of Funds		
Expenditure		
Hospital Services	30,032.8	
Community Services	4,583.8	
Administration	1,400.8	
Other Services	166.4	
	36,183.8	
Less: Income Retained	(291.8)	
Expenses met by		
West Midlands RHA	(1,606.0)	34,286.0
Movement in Working Balances:		
Increase in Stocks	306.8	
Increase in Debtors	185.9	
Decrease in Cash	(481.7)	
Increase in Creditors	(172.1)	
Increase in Earnings Contribution		
Payment Adjustment	(39.9)	(201.0)
		34,085.0
Cash Limit Overspend		48.0
		34,037.0

Reconciliation between 'Cash Limit' Basis and 'Income and Expenditure' Basis

	£000	£000
Overspending – Cash Limit Basis		48.0
Overspending – Income and Expenditure		
Basis (see·page 13)		24.0
		24.0
Represented by:		
Income and Expenditure 1983/84		
Underspending	454.0	
Cash Limit 1983/84 Underspending	(229.0)	
	225.0	
Movement in Working Balances	(201.0)	24.0

Capital Expenditure

Summary of Capital Expenditure 1984/85

	Block £000	Delegated £000	WMRHA £000
Acute Unit			
Manor Hospital			
Development Control Centre	28.8		
Gas Outlets	17.1		
Replacement Chapel/Physiotherapy Department	67.1		
St John's Block	46.4		
Domestic Rest Room Upgrading	43.2		
Pathology Extension	25.6		
Replacement Generator	72.8		
Visitors Toilet Facilities	19.5		
Other Schemes	70.2		
	390.7		
Replacement Incinerator/Heat Recovery		11.9	
Midwifery Training School		7.1	
Canterbury Ward		4.8	
Steam Boiler		4.2	
DGH Staff Location		0.1	
DGH Roadworks		108.1	
		136.2	
Town Wharf Residential Accommodation			0.6
DGH Phase IV			452.8
Out-Patients Department Extension			121.8
			575.2
General Hospital			
Workshops Upgrading	27.1		
New Switchboard	48.5		
Other Schemes	3.8		
	79.4		
Lift Replacement		2.8	
		2.8	
Balances C/fwd	**470.1**	**139.0**	**575.2**

	Block £000	Delegated £000	WMRHA £000
Balances B/fwd	**470.1**	**139.0**	**575.2**
Acute Unit (continued)			
Goscote Hospital			
Nurses Home Upgrading	36.2		
New Switchboard	18.5		
Kitchen Scheme/Autovalet	93.0		
	147.7		
Additional Wards			54.2
Edinburgh Ward Upgrading			1.0
Kitchen and Dining Room			6.4
Geriatric Unit			1.6
			63.2
Mental Handicap Unit			
St Margaret's Hospital			
Lavender Home Sanitary Annexe	99.7		
Maintenance Workshops	31.5		
Roadworks	114.3		
Bore Hole	23.7		
Children's Residential Home	41.6		
Fire Precautions	76.4		
Other Schemes	79.1		
	466.3		
Scarlett Home Sanitary Annexe		85.8	
Yardley Top		13.5	
Other Schemes		0.3	
		99.6	
Great Barr Hall			13.9
Ridge Hill Units			43.3
Clothing Shop Extension			1.5
Heating System Upgrading			0.2
			58.9
Balances C/fwd	**1,084.1**	**238.6**	**697.3**

Revenue Expenditure

Comparison of Budget with Expenditure 1984/85
(Income and Expenditure Basis)

Budget Group	Budget £000	Expenditure £000	Under/Over Spending £000
Hospital Medical & Para-Medical Services:			
Medical Staff	1,372.5	1,411.7	39.2
Medical & Surgical Equipment	915.4	951.8	36.4
Pharmacy	1,086.2	1,067.4	18.8–
Diagnostic Services	1,228.5	1,237.2	8.7
Miscellaneous Services	757.5	749.2	8.3–
Sub-Total	**5,360.1**	**5,417.3**	**57.2**
Community Medical & Para-Medical Services:			
Community Medical Staff	292.5	295.2	2.7
Family Planning	268.1	308.7	40.6
Dental	172.1	164.1	8.0–
Other Para-Medical	525.6	527.3	1.7
Miscellaneous Services	455.0	426.7	28.3–
Sub-Total	**1,713.3**	**1,722.0**	**8.7**
Nursing Services:			
Hospitals	12,376.5	12,272.1	104.4–
Community	2,631.5	2,623.9	7.6–
Sub-Total	**15,008.0**	**14,896.0**	**112.0–**
Operational Services:			
Administration & Medical Records	1,724.3	1,739.8	15.5
Catering	1,717.7	1,724.7	7.0
Domestic	1,755.4	1,745.9	9.5–
Portering	448.5	446.1	2.4–
Laundry	340.5	342.4	1.9
Transport	197.2	180.7	16.5–
Other Supplies Services	483.7	459.3	24.4–
Miscellaneous Services	347.9	369.5	21.6
Sub-Total	**7,015.2**	**7,008.4**	**6.8–**
Estate Management	3,759.1	3,850.4	91.3
District Administrative Services	1,350.0	1,335.6	14.4–
Contingencies	56.3	56.3	—
TOTAL	**34,262.0**	**34,286.0**	**24.0**
Less: Income & Expenditure 1983/84 Underspending	(454.0)		
Add: Cash Limit 1983/84 Underspending	229.0		
Revenue Cash Limit	**34,037.0**		

Cost of Caring

	ACUTE		COMMUNITY		MENTAL HANDICAP		MENTAL ILLNESS	
	Goscote Hospital		Community Health Services		St Margaret's/ Daisy Bank		Bloxwich/Mossley Day Centre	
	1984/85 £000	1983/84 £000	1984/85 £000	1983/84 £000	1984/85 £000	1983/84 £000	1984/85 £000	1983/84 £000
	28	20	563	516	193	186	14	5
	28	26	—	—	50	54	1	3
	896	737	2,481	2,339	4,224	4,131	210	212
	42	33	812	717	270	307	14	12
	5	5	—	—	4	4	2	1
	—	—	254	185	—	—	—	—
	37	13	—	—	100	63	5	27
	1	1	—	—	2	3	—	—
	56	60	—	—	526	598	29	25
	152	132	—	—	681	661	23	22
	166	148	—	—	708	720	18	23
	190	149	—	—	1,216	1,207	31	23
	3	3	—	—	12	9	11	6
	17	16	—	—	169	162	—	—
	1	—	—	—	14	6	—	—
	101	69	904	855	628	698	27	14
	1,723	**1,412**	**5,014**	**4,612**	**8,797**	**8,809**	**385**	**373**
	1984/85	1983/84	1984/85	1983/84	1984/85	1983/84	1984/85	1983/84
	169	153	—	—	796	826	14	14
	136	123	—	—	714	739	10	11
	80%	80%	—	—	90%	90%	71%	79%
	49,640	44,993	—	—	260,503	270,572	3,587	4,035
	655	567	—	—	483	386	122	130
	75.8	79.4	—	—	539.3	701.0	29.4	31.0
	—	—	—	—	2,158	2,500	947	380
	—	—	—	—	—	—	—	—
	—	—	—	—	2,562	2,856	7,065	4,181
	£	£	£	£	£	£	£	£
	34.71	31.62	—	—	33.55	32.05	72.76	66.47
	2,630.53	2,508.87	—	—	18,095.24	22,466.53	2,330.36	2,063.22
	—	—	—	—	11.12	16.71	31.68	20.24
	—	—	—	—	12.88	9.21	23.46	23.03
	—	—	18,924.40	17,334.69	—	—	—	—
	—	—	—	—	—	—	—	—

Capital Expenditure

Summary of Capital Expenditure 1984/85

	Block £000	Delegated £000	WMRHA £000
Balances B/fwd	1,084.1	238.6	697.3
Mental Illness Unit			
Bloxwich Hospital			
Improvements	42.5	0.3	
	42.5	**0.3**	
Ward Conversion			1.8
			1.8
Community Unit			
Clinics – Upgrading programme	34.2		
Other Schemes	20.4		
	54.6		
Community Hospital			87.2
			87.2
Other Schemes			
Computers	256.3		
Medical Equipment	61.5		
Design Fees	257.1		
	574.9		
Batching Continuous Washer		188.0	
Purchase of 2, 6 & 32 Ida Road		15.5	
		203.5	
Miscellaneous			2.4
			2.4
TOTAL EXPENDITURE	1,756.1	442.4	788.7

Trust Funds

Income and Expenditure Account

	1984/85		1983/84	
	£	£	£	£
Income				
Donations	90,822		93,826	
Legacies	11,380		1,500	
Investment Income	30,363		29,470	
		132,565		124,796
Less: Expenditure				
Patients Amenities	91,170		64,343	
Staff Amenities	15,941		22,593	
		107,111		86,936
Surplus for Year		25,454		37,860

Balance Sheet

	1984/85		1983/84	
	£	£	£	£
Accumulated Fund				
Capital in Perpetuity		85,904		85,904
Other Funds				
Special Purposes	107,304		97,219	
General Purposes	126,966		111,597	
		234,270		208,816
		320,174		294,720
Represented by:				
Investments				
Narrower Range	311,086		220,625	
Wider Range	—		50,000	
		311,086		270,625
Current Assets				
Sundry Debtors	24,376		17,061	
Cash at Bank	38,973		12,602	
	63,349		29,663	
Less: Current Liabilities				
Sundry Creditors	54,261		5,568	
		9,088		24,095
		320,174		294,720

External audit

The Audit Branch of the DHSS has the statutory duty of auditing the accounts of health authorities under the National Health Service Act, 1977.

The aims of the audit are to ensure the accounts are correct, complete and lawful, i.e. they 'present fairly' the financial transactions of the authority. The audit also aims to prevent, identify and deter fraud, whilst reviewing the economy and efficiency of the provision of services.

Review by parliament

The audited accounts are sent to the DHSS. The accounts for all health authorities are then summarized and presented to Parliament, where spending levels and statistical comparisons are subject to review by Members of Parliament.

Activity 2	*a* List the financial statements contained in the financial report as shown for the Walsall DHA. *b* Compare the statements with those contained in the annual report of a company. What financial statement is not produced by health authorities?

The financial statements produced by the health authority are:
1 Source and Application of Funds – Revenue
2 Reconciliation between 'Cash Limit' Basis and 'Income and Expenditure' Basis
3 Comparison of Budget with Expenditure
4 Summary of Capital Expenditure
5 Trust Funds, Income and Expenditure Account
6 Trust Funds, Balance Sheet

In comparing the statements with those contained in the annual report of a company you will note that a health authority does not produce a profit and loss account or a conventional balance sheet.

There is a balance sheet for the trust funds but, unlike companies, the NHS does not at present have a system of fixed assets accounting. All hospitals and other buildings administered by the health authority are government property and accounted for by central government.

The sources and applications of funds statement can be considered to be the most important financial statement produced in a health authority financial report as it shows the amount of money allocated to the district health authority and the areas on which the money has been spent.

If a cash limit is overspent, the amount of the overspending reduces the next year's allocation of money. In this way Parliament controls the level of spending within the NHS.

If a cash limit is underspent it may be carried forward up to a maximum 1% of revenue cash allocation. Any underspending over this 1% is lost. Health authorities therefore monitor spending closely throughout the year. Comparison of actual spending with target or budgeted spending is carried out under the supervision of the Chief Financial Officer. The budget is therefore the major factor in controlling spending within a health authority.

Activity 3	Examine the sources and application of funds statement in the financial report you have obtained for a local health authority.

Examine the sources and application of funds statement in the financial report you have obtained for a local health authority.
a Has the authority underspent or overspent its revenue cash allocation?
b Is the cash limit overspent or underspent?

In Activity 2 you should have identified a conventional form of balance sheet for trust funds. Members of fund-raising organizations, e.g. Round Table groups, often make donations to hospitals and clinics to help finance the service and to purchase equipment. Individuals often make these donations as a gesture to show their gratitude for the nursing and care they received during a serious illness or long stay in a particular hospital or clinic.

This money is not the property of the NHS or the health authority. Money received from donations is paid into separate bank and investment accounts. The health authority administers the affairs of the fund as trustee in accordance with guidelines laid down by the government. Accounts which detail the activities of the fund – the income and expenditure account and balance sheet, have to be produced each year.

Generally the donations received by trust funds are invested and the interest earned is used to purchase new equipment or help finance services, thus improving conditions for patients receiving treatment. There are certain restrictions on the type of investments which may be made; these take account of risk and the amount of investment interest likely to be earned.

| Activity 4 | Look again at the accounts of Walsall District Health Authority.
a What is the total value of donations made to the Health Authority?
b What are *narrower range* investments and *wider range* investments?
c What do you think *capital in perpetuity* is?
d Why do you think *other funds* are split between *special purposes* and *general purposes*? |

Guidance to Activity 4 is given over the page, but do not refer to this until you have attempted the activities.

In addition to items purchased from the monies available in the trust fund, organizations or a business may raise funds to purchase an expensive single item of equipment. Local newspapers often publish photographs of the ceremony where equipment purchased in this way is handed over to a hospital.

This block has shown that the National Health Service has to operate using limited financial resources. There is also increasing pressure from central government for health authorities to provide services more efficiently and thus reduce costs.

To enable health authorities and central government to monitor trends in the demand for services and the costs of treating different diseases and different types of patient, each health authority produces annual statistics and unit costs.

Within a health authority unit costs are an important means of financial control: costs of treating the same type of patient in different hospitals can be compared to provide a measure of efficiency and cost control. Comparisons can also be made with previous years.

Nationally, the DHSS monitors the unit costs of health authorities and calculates national average unit costs. The DHSS also issues guidelines on methods of providing services more economically and efficiently, thus reducing the overall cost of providing a National Health Service.

Guidance for Activity 4

The total value of donations received by Walsall DHA is
£320 174.

Narrower range investments include fixed-interest deposits such
as bank deposits, government stocks and company debentures.
Wider range investments include shares in public limited
companies and other investments where the interest rate is not
fixed.

Capital in perpetuity   Some donations are given expressly on
the condition that the money is invested as a whole and only the
income from the investments used to help finance services or
purchase equipment.

When donations are made for any purposes that the trustees
think appropriate, these are called *general purpose funds*. Other
donations are given to provide a particular piece of equipment
or to finance the service of a particular ward: these are *special
purpose funds*.

Block 12
Interviews with People Involved in Finance

This block, unlike the previous ones, involves little active work from you. It gives information about jobs carried out by a variety of people in finance.

Reading this block will help you to understand the wide variety of work that has to be carried out in the finance area. It also gives the comments of people who have real practical experience in jobs that they have been involved in for a considerable time. We can never fully learn through others' experiences, but taking account of what they say can help to create an awareness that will aid our general understanding.

| Activity 1 | Read the following descriptions of jobs by six people in the world of finance. Use these descriptions, and any other sources of information which you can find, to design a leaflet and a poster for a careers convention outlining the opportunities in finance available to school leavers. |

| Activity 2 | The six people who give accounts of their jobs and careers have each taken a different approach in their descriptions. Some 'talk us through' their jobs, giving small details and thoughtful explanations, others give a much more 'formal' account, almost a job description for guidance to potential applicants for jobs. |

Why do you think this difference occurs? Do you think it is to do with the particular positions they occupy, or just a matter of personal style?

1 The accountant 'in practice'

I am a chartered accountant and I work for a large firm of accountants at their office in Manchester city centre.

I spend most of my time on auditing work, that is visiting our clients at their premises to verify and check their accounts. I usually spend anything from a few days to a month on these audits, depending on the size of the task.

Life in a professional office will be as varied as the range of clients that is served. The practice can vary in size from the one or two partner firm to the large international organization employing thousands of people in offices throughout the world. The services offered to clients include the areas below.

a Accountancy	Writing up accounting records and the preparation of financial statements.
b Taxation	Preparation of income tax returns for individuals or corporation tax computations for limited companies.
c Audit	Reporting to shareholders on the 'truth and fairness' of financial statements; this may include a review of internal control procedures within the company.
d Executorship	Executing the terms of a will and administering any subsequent trust funds.
e Insolvency	Winding up a company to ensure that creditors and shareholders share equitably in the remaining assets.

The above covers only the main areas of work in a professional office. The increased complexity of modern businesses has led to specialization in the larger accounting offices and staff may work exclusively in one or other of the above areas.

Students training in a small office are more likely to get a thorough grounding in all aspects of accountancy but should be aware of the correlation between the size of the practice and the likely remuneration!

In recent years, professional offices have introduced 'in-house' computers to either,
a prepare clients' financial statements from incomplete records or,
b to provide other services, such as the preparation of sales invoices, or profit and cash flow forecasts – the latter is an increasingly common area of work (whether a computer is used or not) as banks will often require such forecasts if clients apply for loans or are experiencing financial difficulties.

My duties with the practice have changed over the past few years. I spend more and more time looking at the 'accounting systems' as a whole and less time checking documents such as invoices, receipts and ledger accounts.

As many firms have computerized accounting systems, I need to know something about how their systems work. This does not involve me in programming the computers, but I do need to know how the computer produces accounts from the data fed in. I am particularly interested in the system that gives a check on the accuracy of the records. Most computer systems have a built in 'cross check' to verify information, and I need to look specifically at the efficiency of this aspect.

2 Local authority treasurer

I am employed by a county council. This means that I was appointed to my post of County Treasurer by the elected members of council who represent the interests of the people who live and work in this county.

All local authorities were created by Act of Parliament. Local authorities provide services such as education, social services, policing, etc. Various acts, e.g. the Education Acts, lay down the powers and duties regarding the provision of services.

Local authorities are statutory corporations and can only do those things which they are authorized to do by statute. The way this authority provides an education service has to be in accordance with the provisions of the Education Acts.

The authority cannot spend money or collect income providing any services unless it has the statutory power to do so. However, the council has a discretionary spending power, but this is very limited.

This county will spend £489 million in 1985/86 providing services. The education service is the major service: over £293 million will be spent on providing and maintaining schools and colleges throughout this county in 1985/86.

The money which the authority spends comes from the following sources:
1 *The Government* (in the form of grants),
2 *Rates* (levied on householders and industrialists),
3 *Fees and charges* (levied on such things as college courses).

In 1985/86, £212 million will be received by the county in the form of government grants. To ensure that this money is spent legally, i.e. in accordance with the provisions of acts of parliament, the local authority is required by the Local Government Act, 1972, Section 151, to make a statement of its financial affairs.

My appointment as the 'responsible financial officer' is therefore required by Parliament in order to ensure the money they give to the local authority to finance services is spent legally, and value for money in services is obtained.

I have to account for money spent in a financial year by producing financial accounts for all services provided by the County Council. The Local Government Finance Act, 1982, and the Accounts and Audit Regulations, 1983, lay down the format of these accounts and make provision for an annual External Audit of the accounts of this county, by officers of the Audit Commission. As the 'responsible financial officer', I have to certify that the annual accounts are correct and prepared in accordance with the acts.

Income from rates in 1985/86 will be £211 million; £63 million will be received from fees and charges.

As well as accounting to Parliament for grant money received, I also act as financial steward for money received from the ratepayers of the county.

As responsible financial officer, I have not only to ensure that the money is spent legally, but also that the services are provided efficiently and economically and the risk of fraud and the misappropriation of cash and assets is minimized.

I am therefore accountable to the ratepayers for all money raised to finance services. The Accounts and Audit Regulations, 1983, require me to allow the ratepayers and electors of the county to inspect the annual accounts prior to their publication. A ratepayer/elector for this area can inspect any document, book or record relating to any item of expenditure or income appearing in the accounts.

In order to reduce the risk of loss because of fraud or the misappropriation of cash and assets, and to ensure services are run efficiently and economically, I am required by the Accounts and Audit Regulations, 1983, to maintain a Current Internal Audit of the accounts.

Out of a total staff of 250 in my Treasurer's Department, 20 are employed in the Internal Audit Section.

My main duties as County Treasurer are to provide financial advice to the council regarding the costs of policy options and to provide day-to-day financial services to all council departments.

I have 20 qualified accountants in my department; they are all members of the Chartered Institute of Public Finance and Accountancy.

There is a financial management cycle in local authorities.

The financial year runs from 1 April to the 31 March. The first part of this cycle is to estimate the total cost of running services in the next financial year. This exercise is carried out from November onwards each year. My accountants provide me with estimates split into three main areas:
1 *Capital*   new schools, roads, etc.,
2 *Running costs*   gas, electricity, maintenance, etc.,
3 *Employee costs*.

I then have to discuss these estimates with councillors. As the elected policy-makers, they have to decide spending priorities. . At the present time we are in a situation where, since 1975, successive governments have severely cut the level of grants payable to local authorities. In addition, the government limits the amount of income we can raise from rates.

This county has had to cut costs, and therefore services, in line with government policy. I provide the councillors with costs of alternative options; they may ask me to compare the costs of different methods of constructing a school, calculate the savings from closing classrooms, etc.

My staff, of course, produce all the information for me, but I have to present it to the councillors and await their decisions.

When all the estimates have been finalized, the full council approves the budget and I have the responsibility of monitoring income and expenditure against that budget throughout the financial year.

My staff is responsible for day-to-day financial management of services. The staff of my department is split into sections dealing with services. Each section is headed by a qualified accountant.

These sections are responsible for the payment of invoices for capital and revenue expenditure, monitoring spending, providing budget holders with reports, and producing the final accounts for the service. The financial management cycle ends with the production of the final accounts.

The county employs 28 729 people. I have a large wages and salaries section and a pensions section. The majority of staff in these sections are involved in paying the employees of the county.

Throughout the financial year I have to report regularly to councillors on our spending. I have to ensure that at any time there is enough money in our bank accounts to pay wages, invoices, etc. This may involve the raising of loans or the investment of surplus money. I have a particular interest in the investment work. Pension fund money has to be invested prudently, and I spend a lot of time with investment brokers and attending meetings in the City of London.

I delegate as much as possible the responsibility for day-to-day financial management. However, I maintain overall responsibility and on some issues I have to consult the heads of other departments, such as architects, surveyors and providers of legal services, particularly with regard to costing new capital schemes.

The financial accounting systems in the county are all computerized. The computer is situated in my department and, although my deputy acts as Data Processing Manager, I maintain overall responsibility for the efficient and economic running of the computer section. In addition, no financial system is computerized until it has been approved by me. I employ specialists to develop and write systems, and computer auditors to audit systems to minimize the risk of fraud.

My duties are therefore complex. As well as my financial responsibilities, I like to take an interest in the recruitment of staff, and staff development and training. For senior appointments I will interview candidates myself with a team of other officers and councillors; junior appointments I leave to my deputy.

3 Credit controller

I work for a company which acts as selling and distribution
agents for a German firm which manufactures high fashion
clothes. However, irrespective of the nature of the business, or
whether the credit control function is being performed for
one's own company or for a third party, the basic principles
and activities will be the same.

What is *credit control?* The majority of firms in this day and age
sell on credit, thus allowing their customers a certain time in
which to pay for the goods that they have received. The aim of
credit control is to ensure that these customers pay within that
period of time, whether it be 10 days, 30 days or 6 months, etc.
This is the main activity of credit control, but this in itself
involves several other factors. Customers may return goods for
which they require a credit note. It will fall to the Credit
Control Section to see that these credit notes are raised as
speedily as possible. Many customers will use the fact they have
not received a credit note as a reason for not paying, and in
some cases may be quite entitled to do so.

The Credit Control Section may find itself responsible for
withholding merchandise from customers who despite many
requests for payment simply seem unable to send the cheque! It
is amazing how money somehow materializes out of thin air
when the threat of withholding supplies is applied.

Credit control personnel may find themselves acting as 'stand
in' PR officers for their company. Where a customer has
experienced poor deliveries, faulty goods, incorrect
merchandise, etc., it will often happen that the Credit Control
Section will attempt to calm the situation by offering, for
example, extended credit terms, extra discounts, or the facility
of a payment plan where it is agreed that the customer will pay
stated amounts over a certain period of time (usually outside
the normal credit terms) in order to clear the debt by an agreed
date.

As already stated, credit control is concerned with ensuring that
people pay within the agreed terms. There are several ways in
which this can be achieved. The most common method is a
request for payment by telephone. The telephone has
advantages over the other methods which are described below.
It enables the person carrying out the credit control to get a
'feel' for the customer they are dealing with. If every time you

ring Mr Jones he is 'unavailable because he is in a meeting', 'on holiday', or simply 'has just popped out', you begin to get the impression that there is something not quite right. It is a good policy to make a note of all calls made to customers, with pertinent comments, as these can be invaluable for future use when further action may be requested to collect the debt.

A further advantage of the telephone is that it allows you to obtain a 'contact' within the company and to build up some sort of working relationship with that person. However, care must be taken not to let oneself get too involved, as unscrupulous customers can often try to use this relationship to their own advantage.

Where it is not possible to contact the person concerned by telephone, it then becomes necessary to write to them. These letters may be generated by a computer, which simply highlights overdue amounts, or may be raised on a more personal basis, depending upon the customer, the length of time they have been trading with you, or the amount of the debt involved.

The letters themselves can vary in strength from, 'We would like to draw your attention to the overdue amounts shown below and respectfully request your payment by return of post,' to, 'In the absence of an immediate payment to clear the amount stated, legal action will be taken to recover this debt.'

This brings me to another aspect of credit control: legal action. I personally feel that this is the aspect I like least of all. Not because of the courts and solicitors being involved, but simply because you feel as though you have lost the match. Legal action will only be taken as a last resort, partly because of the costs involved and partly because, as it is the credit controller's responsibility to collect the debt, he or she will generally do everything in their power to do so before resorting to legal action. When a debt is given to a solicitor to collect, it tends to take the reins from your hands. Whilst your solicitor will instruct you in what courses of action are available and ask which one you would prefer to use, it is not quite the same thing as doing it yourself. However, it is possible to use the County Courts in England to collect debts up to a maximum of £5000, and this you can do without the aid of a solicitor.

It is hoped that all these methods will produce just one result: a payment from the customer. Cheques should be arriving on a daily basis as the result of the telephone calls, letters, legal action, etc., and it is vitally important that these are recorded in a clear and concise manner and paid into the bank as quickly as possible. Cheques are not guarantees of payment: they may sometimes 'bounce'. One particular example I recall was of a customer that I dealt with who, because of his bad trading record, sent post-dated cheques to clear his account, to the value of £50 000, and then proceeded to stop every one before it could clear the bank account! When cheques are received, it is imperative that they are allocated to the customer's account as quickly as possible. Customers get very annoyed when you request payment for an item that was paid for several days previously.

But it does sometimes happen that all the procedures tried will not effect payment. A company may go bankrupt, may go into liquidation, etc., or it might be that the costs involved in collecting the debt exceed the actual amount of the debt itself. In these cases it is not financially viable to keep chasing the money. These debts are called *bad debts* and I think the name speaks for itself. It is inevitable that when selling on credit, some customers are not going to pay, or will not be able to pay. Companies therefore make allowances in their accounts for bad debts and it is against this *provision* that these uncollectable amounts will be written off.

One aspect of credit control which does require careful and continued scrutiny is the 'credit' aspect of the 'control'. It is possible through various professional organizations to obtain financial details concerning potential customers. These organizations go under various names, perhaps the most well-known being Dunn–Bradstreet. In addition it is possible to obtain bank references for customers and also to obtain trade references from people who have previously supplied goods to this potential customer. However, these must not be taken as a guarantee that funds are available or that debts will be paid. Bank references tend to be a little ambiguous with comments such as, 'At the present time we see no reason why our client will not be able completely to satisfy this debt'. The part to remember is that you will not be requesting payment at this present time, but sometime in the future. With trade references it is possible that your potential customer will give you the names of two or three 'cultivated' accounts. These are suppliers whom he always pays on time, with no quibbling, and he may even pay early in order to take advantage of any prompt payment discounts. However these may be the only customers he pays promptly! The trade references received from these cultivated accounts will of course be very favourable towards your potential customer! It has been known for people to give as trade references companies which are owned or run by their mothers, fathers, sisters, brothers or lovers! So beware of references and treat them with care.

The real point behind this is not to supply goods to customers whom you consider to be risky. A great many organizations today measure their success by the amount they sell, and my own company is no exception! However as any credit controller will tell you, 'Nothing is sold until it is paid for: it has simply been given away'.

The sales force of any company will be judged by the amount of sales they generate and it is the sales force who will be saying: 'We must supply that customer. We don't have anyone else in the area,' or, 'We must supply them; they've ordered £10 000 worth of goods,' or, 'Yes, we know they are a bit suspect, but I think they will pay in the end.' However, it must be remembered that the sales force will be keeping its eye firmly on its own sales figures, and any bonuses that may be attached, and the fact that the overdue debt may arise through supplying these 'suspect' customers will have very little importance to them. It will, however, be very important to the credit control section. It must be remembered that the credit control function is to control credit, not just collect debts. When firms continue to supply customers who will not pay, despite the arguments of the credit control section, it makes a mockery of the whole system of credit control and thoroughly demotivates the staff involved.

In this present day when cash flow problems abound in many industries, an effective credit control section is the most valuable weapon a firm has in fighting the battle. Used in the correct way, it can prevent a firm from becoming insolvent, and perhaps becoming a bad debt, in someone else's books.

I would like to finish by saying one thing. The problems of credit control have been explained and I do not wish to undervalue them in any way. Despite them, or maybe even because of them, credit control can be an extremely rewarding occupation, and I would recommend it to anyone who enjoys working with figures, talking to people, and who welcomes a continual challenge.

4 *Treasurer of a local cricket club*

As the elected treasurer of my local cricket club, I serve on the management committee together with the Chairman, Secretary, Bar Secretary, Fund-raising Secretary, Social Secretary, Club Captain and two co-opted members.

All except these last two were elected at the Annual General Meeting, and we serve the club for one year. My real title is Honorary Treasurer, meaning that I am not a paid officer of the club. I was elected to the post because the members thought I could do it and I was willing to stand for election.

My role is to look after the financial affairs of the club. I record all the income from bar takings, raffles, subscriptions, match fees and any other events that raise money. I also of course pay out for running expenses, such as rates on our club house and on the necessary operating costs – heating, insurances, purchases of equipment and the purchase of bar stock for re-sale.

Because our club is run by voluntary help, all the officials who form the management committee are unpaid and so are the members who help to run the bar. This keeps our costs down, but it does mean that a lot of people have to give up their free time to help.

During the cricket season visiting teams have teas supplied and must generally be entertained, and of course the playing field needs to be maintained. This costs money and so the players organize raffles and pay match fees, as well as annual subscriptions. This all has to be accounted for.

Because of the voluntary nature of the club and the positions of the officers who run it, it is difficult to force people to do things that have to be done. Unlike working for a firm, there is no real boss and no conditions of service, job descriptions and hours of work. I can only do my job if everyone pulls their weight and helps.

I am very conscious of the need to keep very careful and accurate records. We have to pay Value Added Tax on our purchases and charge Value Added Tax on our sales. This means that every quarter I have to complete returns to Customs and Excise detailing Value Added Tax paid and collected, and then pay over any Value Added Tax balance.

We have had one visit so far from the Customs and Excise Department to check on our system and our records to make sure that we are doing the job properly. Fortunately they decided we were.

We hold management meetings once a month, and each officer reports on the activities. My job is to give up-to-date pictures of the financial situation – what money we have in the bank, what sales we have made over the bar, any outstanding bills, and so on.

From time to time we have liquidity problems. Poor bar sales seem to arise just when we have most to pay for, say equipment repairs or kit for the new season. This involves me in cash planning, and arranging with our bank manager for overdraft facilities. I find he is more sympathetic if I let him know in advance of possible problems, rather than ring him up in a panic at the last minute.

At the end of the year I produce the accounts for the club. These consist of a Bar Trading Account, an Income and Expenditure Account and a Balance Sheet. We have a local accountant who actually prepares the accounting statements from my records. He audits my records and accounts and compiles the accounting statement and of course signs to say that they are a true and fair representation of the club's financial situation.

At the A.G.M. I deliver my report to the members and they often ask questions about the financial situation. They seem generally to look at the money we hold in the bank at the end of the year and compare it with what we held at the beginning. This simple comparison annoys me, because it really tells our members nothing. We spend all year carefully recording income and expenditure; we pay a qualified accountant to produce accounts that give in detail sources of profit earned, assets and liabilities and so on, and simply looking at cash held and money in the bank is a very limited way to view our financial records.

What we also do at the A.G.M. is fix membership subscriptions for the coming year, and I try to give a budget for the year of income and expenditure so that it justifies asking for an increase in subscriptions if that is what we propose.

5 A branch manager within the Nationwide Building Society

Nationwide Building Society is Britain's third largest building society, with assets of over £10 billion. It has an extensive branch network of 529 branches covering England, Scotland, Wales and Northern Ireland.

In view of its size and number of employees, over 4500, it operates on a decentralized basis, that is authority for a great many functions and decisions is given to branch-level staff, unlike a centralized system where branches are collecting stations with work and decisions being passed upwards to head office.

The prime function of a Branch Manager in the Society is to assume responsibility for all aspects of the operation of his branch and by continuous supervision to achieve the highest standards of administration and development in his branch and branch area.

The duties of a Manager are subdivided into various sections: development, staff, mortgage, investment, security, premises and administration.

Development

Development means in simple terms the gaining of more business, be it investment moneys or mortgage lending. This can be achieved by maintaining contact with the Society's agents to realize their potential, by generating investment business through staff training and display material, and by establishing and servicing good business contacts.

Staff

The Branch Manager deals with the recruitment and interviewing of clerical staff and recommends their appointment to head office.

He has to ensure that his staff are well trained in the Society's procedures and are motivated and encouraged to work to their maximum level of effort and ability. The Manager completes an annual assessment form on staff, maintains staff discipline and is responsible for staff welfare.

Mortgage

Mortgage business can be split into two areas: obtaining new mortgage business and administering accounts after completion of the mortgage.

A branch is responsible for dealing with all aspects of the application: instructing the valuer, obtaining references, deciding on the information available to approve the case, issuing the offer, instructing solicitors, setting up the account record on the computer database, drawing the advance cheque and issuing completion papers to the borrowers. A Branch Manager and Assistant Branch Manager can approve cases up to mandated amounts, and in cases above that consider, recommend and forward to the Regional Manager all cases outside their mandate.

When accounts have been completed they have to be administered. This involves dealing with interest rate changes, granting further advances, dealing with second charges, insurance queries and the redemption or paying off of mortgages. The Manager is also responsible for dealing with defaulting borrowers. Initial approaches for payments in arrears are dealt with at the branch and, following liaison with head office, the Branch Manager will instruct solicitors, swear affidavits, attend court, attend evictions and, once a property has been possessed, instruct solicitors in the sale, instruct estate agents, and generally oversee the sale on behalf of the Society.

Investment

The Manager is the highest level of cheque signatory in the branch and is the authorized signatory for all documents to be checked. He has absolute control of all overdrawn investors accounts and controls the issue of investors' pass books, cards and bond certificates.

Security

The Manager is responsible for ensuring the security of the office premises, equipment and all other confidential information, and he has to ensure that staff adhere strictly to the cash and accounting security procedures. He will do this by making checks which will include 'spot-check' till audits, opening and/or checking, and/or signing post, and making periodic checks of pass books.

Premises

Managers must ensure that legislation affecting office premises
is observed. He has to arrange for the cleaning and maintaining
of the branch and see that a satisfactory standard is maintained.
He also assists the Regional Manager and head office in finding
suitable premises for the Society's operations within the branch
area.

Administration

A responsible Branch Manager will keep administrative
expenses to a minimum to allow the effective operation of his
branch. He must keep up to date with local matters, legislation,
and any aspect of the economic situation which will affect the
Society's business. He will initiate and answer personal
correspondence and also attend conferences and courses held by
the Society and outside bodies together with completing any
returns and/or reports which the Society requires.

Authority

The Manager has control of all office expenditure, can
recommend the appointment of agents and investment
representatives, has a mortgage mandate and a cheque
signatory mandate and has the authority to take actions on his
personal accountability which may be contrary to procedure
but are taken to preserve goodwill.

6 A bank manager

I am the manager of a branch of a bank. Our office is small,
comprising some six tills, a general administrative area, a
secure area which includes the strong room, and my office. The
branch has an established staff of twelve people and, until we
move into new premises or extend our present site, my
Assistant Manager has to work in an open plan office area with
the other staff. This is a good way of supervising staff for most
of the time, but it does restrict the opportunity for me to
delegate much of my interviewing duties to him or her. Having
said that the branch is a small one, it may surprise you to
discover that we hold about 11 000 accounts, dealing with
funds of more than £13 000 000 and loans in excess of
£3 000 000. In the world of the finance industry, such figures are

small fry, and outsiders find it hard to relate them to their
everyday experience.

A typical day

8.30 a.m. Arrive at the branch and open up, unless one of my
senior staff gets there first. The security system, for which I
have overall responsibility, allows me to start work on
outstanding correspondence and other administration
whenever I need to be in the branch.

8.45 a.m. A computer report lists all responses. Responses are
cheques which have been drawn by customers beyond their
means or beyond their allowed overdraft limit. In a small
branch like mine, the manager deals with all lending and so I
have to decide what to do about these cheques. In about 80% of
all cases they have been written just before a salary has been
paid in, or because of some accidental circumstance. In this case
a standard letter is sent to inform the customer and the matter is
soon cleared up. When the spending appears to be deliberately
beyond the means of the customer, the cheque is returned to
the drawer and this usually takes longer to sort out between the
bank, the customer, and the person or organization to whom
the cheque was written.

9.00 a.m. Before the doors open to the public I deal with some
of the personnel matters which are my responsibility. My staff
work a system of job rotation, both between jobs within a
branch and between local branches. This means that they
should not be in the same job long enough to become bored. It
is also left to me to arrange the working day for the staff.
Providing they work 36 hours, it is left to the branch manager
to arrange a schedule which suits everyone but also provides a
satisfactory service for customers. This involves a staggered
lunch hour, earlier starts for some and later finishes for others. I
am not responsible for the appointment of my own staff, as a
central personnel department advertises, selects staff and then
allocates them to branches within the limits of the
establishment allowance. This and other matters of branch
administration occupy me until opening time.

9.30 a.m. Having supervised the opening of the branch, I
usually start on a series of appointments with customers. These
often take up the whole of my day until branch closing time.
The appointments are with customers requiring loans, those

with overdraft problems, clients wishing to make large deposits, those opening business accounts, some requiring advice on gilt funds and other investments, and even authors of textbooks asking me about the nature of my work! In a small branch like mine, all the customers expect to see the manager and this is an important part of the service which we offer.

12.30 p.m. Just before going to lunch I must deal with some applications for cheque guarantee cards and credit cards. These are some of the most important decisions I make since the issue of such a card to the wrong person could cost the bank a lot in bad debts. By referring to the application form and/or previous customer records, I am able to make a balanced judgement of who is able to handle such a facility in a responsible manner. We also monitor the use of such cards to check that previously reliable customers are not suddenly overstretching themselves.

12.45 p.m. I am meeting a good client with business connections for lunch today. Part of my job is to make the business in the branch grow, and so I must cultivate business connections with estate agents, property developers, garage owners, and other business people who may introduce new clients to us. Some of these connections pay dividends almost immediately, while others may have only long-term benefits. Together with providing a friendly and efficient service in the bank, this type of activity forms the marketing function of my job, enabling me to meet growth targets set by head office.

2.30 p.m. Having returned from a very pleasant lunch, I spend some time dealing with minor administrative matters. I phone the station to check on travelling times for the course which I must attend next week. I have to go to these courses or seminars about four times a year, sometimes on a regional basis, sometimes at the bank's national training centre. While I am away, keeping up with the latest technology or management techniques, my assistant manager looks after the branch.

I also find on my desk two passport photographs to sign (bank managers are some of the few people authorized to verify these), and a query regarding the safety of the new kettle in the kitchen (I have overall responsibility for Health and Safety Regulations within the branch).

3.00 p.m. One of the staff with secretarial skills helps me deal with the correspondence for the day. All the standard letters have already been produced and only require signature. The few special cases are now dealt with in time to catch the last post. These include what we call 'status enquiries', requests from other lenders for references on our customers. All banks and financial institutions obtain these for their own protection, and to avoid 'cross-firing': the borrowing of money from one institution to service a loan from another.

3.30 p.m. Last two interviews of the day.

4.30 p.m. General administration and supervision of the end–of–day balancing operations. I am responsible for the security of cash by monitoring staff on a spot-check basis. With the amount of cash handled by our staff, every system must be subject to the human element and the reputation of the bank depends on the integrity of the staff. There has never been any unsavoury incident in a branch which I have managed, but one must remain vigilant with so much at stake.

5.45 p.m. An early finish tonight. I lock up together with the Assistant Manager. Just before I close the office I make a note to draw up a timetable for the staff appraisals which start at the beginning of next month. We appraise the performance of staff every three months, the Assistant Manager being responsible for training and staff development and handling most of these appraisals. Once a year it is my duty to review the progress of each member of staff.

My job is interesting and varied. I receive the benefits of having undertaken a lengthy training but I must also bear the responsibility. I would happily recommend the work to anyone with an eye for detail, a sense of responsibility and integrity, an appetite for hard work, and a wish to serve the interests of both customers and shareholders.

Glossary

Accounting, accountancy

The recording, analysis, and presentation of financial data relating to the transactions of an organization in a form which conforms to the practices and conventions of the accountancy profession. All activities relating to the financial aspects of an organization, with regard to historical data, control of current financial matters and financial planning for the future.

Accountant

A person involved in the practice of accountancy. The term should only be applied to a person who has successfully completed the examinations and practical experience requirements of one of the four professional accountancy institutes. These are the Institute of Chartered Accountants (ICA), the Chartered Association of Certified Accountants (ACA), the Chartered Institute of Management Accountants (CIMA), and the Chartered Institute of Public Finance and Accountancy (CIPFA). Others working in the areas of finance and accountancy may be qualified as members of the Association of Accounting Technicians (AAT). Accountants tend to specialize in either financial accounting or cost and management accounting.

Accounting concepts and conventions

The name given to a series of accepted principles and practices relating to the recording and analysis of financial data, which should be followed in the preparation of all financial statements.

Accruals, or matching, principle

Costs and revenues should be accounted for in the period in which they occur, regardless of when cash changes hands. Any payment in advance for an expense should be excluded from the expenses charged against a particular accounting period, and any amount owing for an expense should be included in the charges made for the period. In this way the profits for a period cannot be manipulated by adjusting the date of payment.

Business entity

Any business is deemed to have an identity which is distinct and separate from that of its owner(s). Financial matters relating to the owner's personal affairs must be kept separate from the business finances at all times.

Consistency convention

Once an accountancy policy has been established by an organization it should be used consistently unless there is good reason for a change. For example, the method of depreciation chosen by a firm should not be changed frequently but should be used consistently.

Cost concept

Assets acquired by an organization should initially be valued at cost, regardless of the apparent market value of the item. If an organization believes it has bought an asset at a bargain price, it should still appear in the books at cost and not at the value which the organization places on it.

Going concern principle

Books of account should always be prepared on the assumption that the organization is going to continue trading. The affairs of the organization should not appear differently if changes in size, ownership, structure, type of business or style of trading, are planned for the near future.

Materiality principle

Items which are to be used over a period of time, but which cost only a small amount, will be charged to the period in which they are bought and will not be treated as fixed assets. It would not be appropriate, for example, to treat pencils, rubbers and rulers as fixed assets and therefore to depreciate them over a number of accounting periods. The purchase of this kind of item will simply be charged as an expense in the stationery account.

Money measurement concept

Only items which can be measured in money terms will be shown in the accounts. One of the greatest assets of an organization might be the skills, knowledge and experience of its staff, but since this cannot be valued precisely in money terms it does not appear in the books.

Prudence convention

When a choice has to be made regarding asset values, liability values or estimated expenses, the accountant will always choose that value which shows the organization in the least favourable light. This convention of caution, conservatism and prudence ensures that the true and fair views which the accounts should present do not overstate the well-being of the firm and thus mislead investors or others dealing with it. For example, stock should always be valued at cost or net realizable value, whichever is the lower, thus ensuring that it does not appear at an unrealistically high value in the balance sheet.

Realization concept

Profit is deemed to occur when a sale takes place and not when cash changes hands. Thus if a transaction is on credit the sale is accounted for as having occurred when the goods change hands, and a debt is then formed between buyer and seller which, when settled at a later date, does not produce any profit.

Acid test ratio
   See **Liquid assets ratio**

Assets

An asset is an item with a reasonable financial value which is owned by an organization.

Current assets

Current assets are items which are owned by the organization but which are constantly changing in nature and/or amount. Most organizations classify their current assets as stock, debtors, prepayments, balance at bank, and cash in hand.

Fixed assets

Fixed assets are those items which an organization expects to keep for a long time to assist in its activities, such as buildings, vehicles and machinery. An item is treated as a fixed asset if the organization would not normally expect to trade in such items frequently.

Auditing

Auditing is the process of checking and verifying accounting documents and statements to ensure that they give a 'true and fair' view of the financial affairs of the organization by independent accountants whose competence and integrity give the required credibility to the financial information report.

Average rate of return

A method of assessing the profitability of a proposed project or operation. The average profit per annum is expressed as a percentage of the average capital employed during the life of the project. This enables the manager to rank competing projects in order of predicted profitability. The percentage average rate of return (sometimes known as the **book rate of return**) is calculated as (C.E. = Capital Employed):

$$\frac{\text{Average rate}}{\text{of return}} = \frac{\text{Average annual profit}}{(\text{Opening C.E.} + \text{Close C.E.}) \div 2} \times 100\%$$

The main weakness of this method of assessing projects is that it ignores the time value of money (which is taken into account when using discounting methods).

Balance sheet

The document which shows the current financial state of an organization. It includes all assets and liabilities of an organization at a given point in time. The account is balanced because capital, the third category of item shown on the balance sheet, is defined as *assets less liabilities*. Thus by displaying assets on one side, opposite capital and liabilities, the accounting equation (capital = assets *less* liabilities) makes the two sides of the balance sheet equal.

The balance sheet is an important document when interpreting the financial affairs of an organization, especially with respect to liquidity, capital structure and gearing.

Bank reconciliation statement

A calculation which reconciles the bank balance shown in an organization's books with that shown on the bank statement.

The two figures will rarely coincide because of delays in the presentation of cheques, the transmission of data between bank and client, and various other reasons.

Regular reconciliation of the figures is an important aspect of cash control in any organization.

Bank statement

A document produced by a bank showing all transactions relating to a client's account. It is an extract from the client's account in the bank's bookkeeping system.

Book rate of return
See **Average rate of return**

Break-even analysis, break-even chart

The name given to a set of techniques which analyses the behaviour of costs in relation to the level of activity in an organization and establishes the levels required to break even, i.e. to make no loss and no profit. The chart is a useful planning device when using marginal costing techniques to predict the effects of various possible levels of price, cost and volumes of output in future accounting periods.

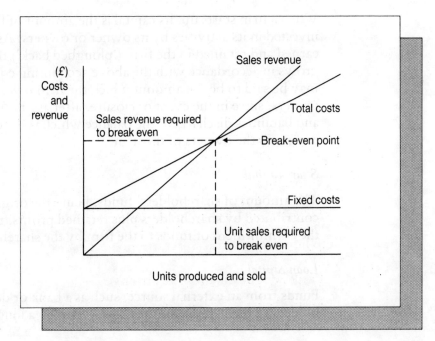

Example of a break-even chart.

Budgets, budgeting

A budget is a financial statement or plan which is prepared and approved in advance of an accounting period. It may not be a forecast of what is expected to happen but rather a target or objective at which the organization should aim. During the accounting period to which the budget applies, comparison is made between the budget and the actual results attained in order to monitor financial performance.

The CIMA defines budgetary control as, 'The establishment of budgets relating the responsibility of executives to the requirements of a policy, and the continuous comparison of actual with budgeted results, either to secure by individual action the objective of that policy or to provide a basis for its revision'. Thus the monitoring of actual performance and its comparison with the budget is designed to allocate responsibility and increase the accountability of individuals within an organization.

One particularly important section of the budget is the cash budget. This plans an organization's inflows and outflows of cash in order to establish any needs for overdrafts or other forms of borrowing during the coming accounting period.

Capital   Capital = Total assets *less* total liabilities.

When a firm starts up, its capital is the amount of funds invested in its activities by its owner or owners. As profits are earned and retained in the firm ('ploughed back') the capital grows in accordance with the above accounting equation. It may be said to be the amount which the firm owes to its owners, since in the event of closure, after assets are realized and liabilities discharged, the balance which is the capital reverts to the owners of the firm.

Share capital

The amount of shareholders' funds, being the original amount contributed by shareholders plus retained profits, representing the commitment of funds to the firm by the shareholders.

Loan capital

Funds from an external source, such as a bank or debenture holders, which are committed to the firm on a long-term basis.

Despite being an external liability for the firm, the term capital is still applied to such loans because of the long-term nature of the commitment.

Capital expenditure

Expenditure on fixed assets or on the improvement of fixed assets in such a way as to increase their value. Expenditure is capitalized if its cost is included in the balance sheet and then subjected to depreciation procedures, rather than being simply charged to the manufacturing, trading or profit and loss accounts for the period as revenue expenditure.

See also **Revenue expenditure**.

Cash book

The cash book consists of a combination of the records of cash in hand and the current bank account of an organization. All receipts and payments related to cash or bank balances are recorded in the book, which forms part of the overall double-entry bookkeeping system. It is a particularly important document in relation to the control of cash, and the reconciliation of records kept by the organization with those held by the bank. This reconciliation of the cash book balance with the bank statement is called a **bank reconciliation statement**.

Club accounts

Accounts of clubs, societies and other non-profit making organizations are kept in a form similar to that used by commercial organizations. Although the format of the accounts is substantially the same, the titles change.

Commercial organization	Club or society
Cash book	Receipts and payments account
Trading account	Trading account
Profit and loss account	Income and expenditure account
Balance sheet	Statement of affairs

These accounts are normally kept by the club treasurer or drawn up by an accountant annually and then presented to the Annual General Meeting of the club for approval by the members.

Cost of goods sold

A figure calculated in the trading account of organizations by adjusting purchases for changes in stock levels.

$$\text{Cost of goods sold} = \text{Opening stock} + \text{Purchases} - \text{Closing stock}$$

This figure is then deducted from sales for the period to calculate gross profit.

$$\textbf{Sales} - \textbf{Cost of goods sold} = \textbf{Gross profit}$$

Cost accounting, costing

The branch of accounting which deals with the ascertainment, analysis, classification and monitoring of costs in an organization. It is closely related to the use of budgets as financial targets and the monitoring of subsequent actual figures in order to compare them.

Cost behaviour

The classification of costs according to their values at different levels of activity. This classification forms the basis for the technique of break–even analysis.

Fixed costs are those which stay the same over a wide range of activity levels, such as rent, rates or insurance.

Variable costs are those which vary in direct proportion to the activity level, such as direct materials, packaging costs or machine power costs.

Semi-variable costs are those which contain elements of both fixed and variable costs. In most organizations for example, electricity costs have a basic fixed element, relating to lighting and heating of the premises even during very low activity periods, and a variable element relating to power used to run machinery. Overall the cost of electricity is then said to be a semi-variable cost.

Stepped costs are those costs which are fixed for small ranges of activity level but which then change in a sudden discrete step. For example, a firm may find that it can operate with a simple delivery van up to about 30% of its normal activity level, but that immediately this level is exceeded another van must be used. Depreciation of these vans would therefore be classified as a stepped cost.

Credit sales

Sales in which the goods or services are delivered but payment is delayed until a later date. The seller of the goods or services becomes a **creditor** of the person or organization to whom they are sold until payment is made.

Creditor

See **Credit sales**

Current ratio

A measure of the liquidity of an organization. The ratio compares the value of current assets with current liabilities to establish the ability of an organization to cover its short-term liabilities. It is usually interpreted in conjunction with the liquid assets ratio and is calculated as follows:

$$\textbf{Current ratio} = \frac{\textbf{Current assets}}{\textbf{Current liabilities}} : \textbf{1}$$

It is generally reckoned that the ratio should be a value of about 2 : 1. A much lower ratio indicates possible problems with meeting liabilities in a hurry, while a much higher ratio indicates that funds are not being used effectively.

Debenture

A loan made to a limited company in exchange for which a debenture certificate is issued and an annual fixed interest charge is paid. Although often confused with them, debentures are not shares and do not imply any ownership rights in the company. The certificates once issued may change hands at some market price, but this does not change the liability of the company. The liability of the company continues to be the amount of the original loan.

Debtor

A person or organization who owes money to another person or organization. The amount of the debt is shown as a current asset in the balance sheet of the person or organization to whom the money is owed. Debtors are treated as liquid assets when assessing the liquidity of an organization as they may be turned into cash quickly should the need arise. Debts of debtors who fail to pay are known as **bad debts**.

Depreciation

The term given to the reduction in book value of a fixed asset charged as an expense to the profit and loss account. It is not a transfer of funds but a non-cash book transfer which enables the cost of fixed assets to be spread evenly through their useful life. When the accumulated depreciation charged against an asset is deducted from the original cost, the remainder is known as the **book value**.

$$\textbf{Book value} = \frac{\textbf{original}}{\textbf{cost of asset}} - \frac{\textbf{accumulated depreciation}}{\textbf{already charged}}$$

The accumulated depreciation to date is shown as a deduction from the appropriate class of fixed assets in the balance sheet.

Discounting methods

A series of techniques for the appraisal of capital investment projects which evaluates costs and revenues taking into account the time value of money. Because money can earn interest over time, cash received sooner is worth more than cash received later. By taking into account the interest which earlier receipt could earn, or **discounting**, future costs and receipts may be expressed in **present value** terms, thus making easier comparison of competing projects. Such **discounted cash flow** techniques include the calculation of a percentage rate of return for a capital investment which takes into account the timing of all payments and receipts relating to the project. The percentage measure is known as the **internal rate of return**.

Expenses

Expenses, or business expenses, are costs charged against gross profit in the profit and loss account of an organization.

When deducted from gross profit, the remainder is net profit.

All expenses may be classified as overheads and are normally sub-divided into administrative expenses, selling and distribution expenses, and financial expenses. Financial expenses are interest charges and other costs directly related to the provision of external funds to finance the organization. The analysis, monitoring and control of expenses is one of the main functions of cost accounting.

Final accounts

The term referring to the accounts produced by an organization at the end of an accounting period in order to calculate profit or loss and then to update the balance sheet. The final accounts include a manufacturing account and trading account, a profit and loss account and, when appropriate, an end of period balance sheet. The equivalent accounts for a club or society or a public sector organization are also sometimes referred to as final accounts.

Fixed costs
See **Cost behaviour**

Gearing

Gearing is a term which relates fixed capital, such as preference shares, debentures, and other loans, with ordinary share capital, or equity capital, which attracts variable percentage dividends. A highly geared company is one with a high proportion of fixed interest capital, whereas a company with low gearing has a high proportion of ordinary share capital. Thus a highly geared company is committed to making a large amount of profit simply in order to cover interest payable on its fixed-interest finances.

Gross profit

Gross profit is the difference between sales revenue and cost of sales. It is the simple profit made from trading, representing the amount by which the trader has marked up goods purchased or manufactured before selling them. It is calculated in the trading account of an organization and represents profit before the deduction of business expenses.

$$\text{Sales} - \text{Cost of sales} = \text{Gross profit}$$

$$\text{Gross profit} - \text{Expenses} = \text{Net profit}$$

Gross profit as a percentage of sales

A measure of profitability expressing the proportion of a trader's turnover which is profit made from increasing the price of bought or manufacturing goods.

$$\text{Gross profit as a percentage of sales} = \frac{\text{Gross profit}}{\text{Sales}} \times 100\%$$

This measure is sometimes referred to as the **gross margin**. As a single measure it has little meaning and must be compared with previous percentages made by organizations undertaking similar business activities.

Income and expenditure accounts
See **Club accounts**
Interpretation of accounts

The techniques of deriving meaning from accounting statements. By examining the accounts and calculating accounting ratios which measure profitability, liquidity and activity, an assessment can be made of the financial performance and status of an organization during an accounting period and at any given time. When interpreting accounts, three comparisons are normally possible:

a Comparison with absolute or generally accepted values for certain ratios, such as the recommended 1:1 level for the liquid assets ratio.
b Comparison with the performance of the same organization during other accounting periods, thus showing changes and trends in the performance of the organization.
c Comparison with other similar organizations.

Insolvency

The condition when the external liabilities of an organization exceed its assets, leading to a negative capital figure on the balance sheet. It is an offence for a business or company to trade when knowingly insolvent. When creditors make claims in law against such a business or company it may lead to bankruptcy and liquidation respectively.

Liquid assets ratio (*also known as* **Acid test ratio** *or* **Quick assets ratio**)
A liquidity ratio which compares current liabilities with the funds which might easily be made available to meet them.

$$\text{Liquid assets ratio} = \frac{\text{Current assets } \textit{less } \text{stock}}{\text{Current liabilities}} : 1$$

It is generally recommended that the value of this ratio should be about 1 : 1. If it is much higher than this, funds are not being used to best advantage. If it is significantly lower than 1 : 1, the organization may have difficulty in meeting current liabilities quickly, should the need arise.

Liquidity ratios

Accounting ratios designed to indicate the current status of an organization in relation to its external liabilities and its ability to meet its debts if required. The main liquidity ratios are the **current ratio** and the **liquid assets ratio**. Liquid funds are those which are most like cash in that they are easily exchangeable for goods or services.

Mortgage

A loan provided to an individual or organization which is secured against a specific property, normally a house or other building. The lender has first claim to the property in the event of a default on the loan, bankruptcy of the individual borrower, or liquidation of a borrowing company.

Net present value

A term relating to discounting techniques for project appraisal. The net present value of revenue is its value taking into account all costs, with both costs and revenues having been discounted to take account of the time value of money. If the net present value of a project is positive at a given rate of discount, this indicates that the project is producing a percentage rate of a return higher than the discount rate.

Net profit

The residual revenue for a period after taking into account all costs. It is calculated in the profit and loss account at the end of an accounting period by deducting expenses from gross profit.

$$\textbf{Net profit} = \textbf{Gross profit } \textit{less} \textbf{ Expenses}$$

It is regarded as an extremely important measure of an organization's perfomance in that it measures its earnings for the period after having met all expenses. It is the figure on which the tax liability for a business is calculated.

Net profits as a percentage of capital employed (*also known as* return on capital employed)

A profitability ratio which measures the earnings of an organization in relation to the funds which it is using.

$$\text{Net profit as a percentage of capital employed} = \frac{\text{Net profit}}{\text{Capital employed}} \times 100\%$$

The capital employed figure used should be an average of
capital employed at the start of the year and that at year end.
Calculation of this ratio is further complicated if interest on
long-term loans has been deducted when calculating net profit.
In this case, such interest should be added back into net profit
before making the calculation. Once calculated, the percentage
should compare favourably with that earned by capital
elsewhere. For example, if a similar amount were placed on
deposit in a bank, a rate close to the bank rate could be earned
with minimal risk. Thus a commercial, risk-taking
organization will normally expect to produce a return on
capital employed in excess of such a percentage.

Net profit as a percentage of sales

A performance ratio which expresses the profit margin of an
organization after taking into account all costs.

$$\text{Net profit as a percentage of sales} = \frac{\text{Net profit}}{\text{Sales}} \times 100\%$$

Such a measure has no meaning on its own but is useful when
compared with previous performances of the same
organization or with other organizations of a similar nature. It
is often read in conjunction with **gross profit as a percentage
of sales** to indicate the extent to which expenses reduce the
margins being earned in trading.

Operating statement
  See **Profit and loss account**

Overheads

A term given to those costs which are neither direct material,
direct labour nor direct expense costs. They are operating
expenses of the business and their cost behaviour may be either
as fixed costs or variable costs. In terms of management control
they are often the target for special attention since they may, if
not carefully managed, account for a disproportionately high
amount of the organization's costs. One cost accounting
technique of **full absorption costing** will require all overhead
costs to be allocated or apportioned to specific parts of the
business operation so that these costs can be spread into the cost
of individual jobs or units of production.

Payback period

A method of evaluating investment projects which assesses the time which it takes for cash inflows to pay back the initial cash outflows on an investment. Organizations often prefer projects with a short payback period, and the technique may be used as a method of sifting out those projects which take a particularly long time to pay back, remaining projects being ranked by other means. As a sole method of project appraisal, its biggest disadvantage is that it ignores all returns beyond the payback date.

Prepayments

Expenses paid for in advance of the accounting period to which they refer. Some expenses, such as rates and insurance, are generally payable in advance. Because of the accounting principle of matching revenue and cost for a period, advance payments are not counted against profit in the expenses figure used in the profit and loss account. Instead the amount paid in advance appears in the balance sheet as a current asset, as the organization is owed a service by the person or organization to whom the prepayment was made.

Profit and loss account

Part of the final accounts of an organization drawn up at the end of each accounting period. The profit and loss account starts with the gross profit and deducts business expenses in order to establish the net profit. A version of the profit and loss account is sometimes called an **operating statement**. The equivalent account in the case of a club or society is known as an **income and expenditure account**.

Profitability

The extent to which an organization makes satisfactory earnings from its operations. Net profit, and in some cases gross profit, is compared with other figures in order to assess the performance of the organization. The main ratios measuring profitability are **gross profit as a percentage of sales, net profit as a percentage of sales** and **net profit as a percentage of capital employed**.

Quick assets ratio *See* **Liquid assets ratio**

Rate of stock turnover

An activity ratio which measures the speed at which an organization sells its stock.

$$\textbf{Rate of stock turnover} = \frac{\textbf{Cost of sales}}{\textbf{Average stock}}$$

This rate indicates the number of times in a given period that the shelves are notionally cleared. A fast rate of stock turnover means that the gross profit margin is being achieved on more occasions in each accounting period. When read in conjunction with the gross profit as a percentage of sales ratio, it indicates a style of trading. Some businesses aim to achieve a large margin on each sale, even if this means that sales are relatively infrequent (high margin, slow turnover), whereas others are happy to make a small profit on each of a large number of sales (low margin, fast turnover).

Ratio analysis

A technique used in the interpretation of accounts which makes comparisons between figures in a given set of accounts, or between the same figure in various sets of accounts, in order to judge the financial performance of the organization. The main groupings of ratios are **activity ratios, liquidity ratios** and **profitability ratios**.

Return on capital employed
See **Net profit as a percentage of capital employed**

Revenue expenditure

Day-to-day expenses of an organization which are charged to the revenue accounts (manufacturing, trading and profit and loss accounts) for the period in which they occur. In contrast **capital expenditure** is the expenditure on fixed assets which are expected to be used within the organization for some considerable time in the future.

Sales to capital employed

An activity ratio which relates the amount of business

transacted by an organization to the amount of funds invested in it.

$$\text{Sales to capital employed} = \frac{\text{Sales}}{\text{Capital employed}}$$

There is no set level for such a ratio, but it may be monitored in order to trace trends of activity within an organization or else to compare it with the ratios of similar organizations.

Semi-variable costs
See **Cost behaviour**

Share Capital

This may be sub-divided as follows:

Authorized capital The amount of funds which may be supplied to a company in exchange for part ownership as defined in the memorandum and articles of association.

Issued share capital Funds actually supplied by the shareholders and used for the purchase of assets to enable business to take place. The capital may be contrasted with **loan capital** which is provided from sources other than the owners of the company.

Standard accountancy practice

An agreed set of principles and conventions which enables accountants to communicate effectively with one another, and to give a true and fair view of the financial affairs of an organization. Details of the accepted practice are contained in a series of **Statements of Standard Accountancy Practice** (SSAP) which provide concise guidelines on formats, principles and conventions. *See also* **Accounting concepts and conventions**

Stepped costs
See **Cost behaviour**

Stock

Stock is the name given by a firm to goods held which it subsequently hopes to sell or to convert into a saleable product. In a trading organization it consists simply of goods bought for resale. In a manufacturing concern, it may refer to raw materials, work in progress or finished goods. In all cases stock should be valued at cost or market value, whichever is the lower, in accordance with the accounting convention of prudence.

Stock–turn ratio
See **Rate of stock turnover**

Trading account

An account which forms part of the group of financial statements called the **final accounts**; it summarizes transactions for an accounting period. The trading account is used for the calculation of gross profit by deducting cost of goods sold from sales. The equation of the trading account is:

$$\textbf{Sales } \textit{less} \textbf{ Cost of goods sold} = \textbf{Gross profit}$$

Cost of goods sold is found by applying a stock adjustment to purchases:

$$\textbf{Opening stock } \textit{add} \textbf{ Purchases } \textit{less} \textbf{ Closing stock} = \textbf{Cost of goods sold}$$

The trading account follows the manufacturing account and precedes the profit and loss account in the final accounts.

Variable costs
See **Cost behaviour**

Index